The

AWAKENING
COURSE

The
AWAKENING
COURSE

The Secret to Solving All Problems

JOE VITALE

WILEY

John Wiley & Sons, Inc.

Published by John Wiley & Sons, Inc., Hoboken, New Jersey.
Published simultaneously in Canada.

For general information on our other products and services or for technical support, please
contact our Customer Care Department within the United States at (800) 762-2974, outside
the United States at (317) 572-3993 or fax (317) 572-4002.

Wiley also publishes its books in a variety of electronic formats. Some content that appears in
print may not be available in electronic books. For more information about Wiley products,
visit our web site at www.wiley.com.

Library of Congress Cataloging-in-Publication Data:

Vitale, Joe, 1953-
   The awakening course : the secret to solving all problems / Joe Vitale.
     p. cm.
   ISBN 978-0-470-88803-2 (cloth); ISBN 978-0-470-94866-8 (ebk);
   ISBN 978-0-470-94867-5 (ebk); ISBN 978-0-470-94868-2(ebk);
   1. Success. 2. Wakefulness. 3. Transcendence (Philosophy) 4. Life skills. I. Title.
   BJ1611.2.V585 2010
   158—dc22

                                   2010032312

Printed in the United States of America

10 9 8 7 6 5 4 3 2 1

To my Mother and Father
Thank you for the gift of life.

No problem can be solved from the same level of consciousness that created it.
—Albert Einstein

Contents

Acknowledgments

Suzanne Burns, my publicist and executive administrator, edited this book from the transcripts to my audio program of the same name. Many others helped in the process, not the least of whom was Nerissa, my life partner, who took care of the critters so I could focus on creating this book. I have many inner circle supporters in my life, a few of whom include Pat O'Bryan, Craig Perrine, Bill Hibbler, Rick and Mary Barrett, Brad Marcus, and Victoria Belue Schaefer. I also want to thank Peter Wink and Theresa Pushkar for their help in creating the course. There's a long list of prosperity teachers who have influenced me, including Reverend Ike, Catherine Ponder, Joseph Murphy, Edwene Gaines, Eric Butterworth, Charles Fillmore, Elizabeth Towne, William Walker Atkinson, Robert Collier, Neville Goddard, Vernon Howard, Stuart Wilde, Terri Cole Whittaker, and Bob Proctor. Many spiritual teachers have also helped, including Rajneesh, Bryon Katie, David Hawkins, and Dr. Hew Len. I also want to thank the fine people at John Wiley & Sons, Inc., particularly Matt Holt, for believing in me and publishing my recent books. If I've forgotten anyone instrumental in creating this book, please forgive me. I am grateful for all of you, including you, the reader. Without you, this book wouldn't be necessary. Please enjoy it, and live long and prosper. Onward to our awakening!

Introduction

In my book, *Zero Limits,* I said there were three stages of awakening. At that time I didn't know there was a fourth stage. I've now experienced it. It's the level of transcendence that Einstein and numerous spiritual teachers spoke of and often lived in. It's as real as your experience of reality right now, but it goes beyond anything you've ever experienced before.

This book goes beyond all my previous work. It goes beyond the hit movie *The Secret,* beyond *The Attractor Factor,* even beyond *Zero Limits.* It builds on them, of course, as the earlier works spoke of the early stages of awakening. But because I had yet to experience the fourth stage, I could not write about it. Until now.

In 2009 I recorded an audio program called *The Awakening Course.* I had no idea if anyone would want it, let alone understand it. To my surprise and delight, it became a bestseller. I had to reprint the course numerous times. People from all over the world were listening to it and "awakening" to new levels. People who were having problems discovered the secret to solving all problems.

As a result of the course's popularity, I decided to turn it into a book. The result is what you are now holding. May it liberate you from all problems and lead you to the happiness you seek—the very happiness that is at the heart of your own awakening.

Chapter 1

What to Expect

Aude aliquid dignum. *(Dare something worthy.)*

—Latin motto, sixteenth century

What would you dare to do if you couldn't lose? What would you dare to be if you were guaranteed unconditional success? What would you dare to have if there were absolutely no limits? What would you dare?

It's time to dare something worthy. Welcome to *The Awakening Course*. Whether you're an avid follower of my message or are new to my personal development regimen, congratulations. By taking this first step, you have opened your life to limitless possibilities.

Where you are right now can be a painful place. I've been there. I have relatives who are still there. I'm doing my best to help them by teaching them what I've learned over the past 20 to 30 years. This is material that I've learned the hard way. When I was homeless, I would go to the library and read books. *The Magic of Believing* by Claude Bristol was amazingly influential in my life, and I read other books such as *Think and Grow Rich*. Thank God for the library. The abundance, the wisdom is right there. I would listen to audio programs like the ones I borrowed from the library as I drove around in Houston, where I was living, where a lot of this took place, where a lot of my first transformations took place. I would make it my "university on wheels," and I would listen and grow and ask myself questions.

This, Too, Shall Pass

What I want you to realize is that where you are right now is temporary. Where you are right now is just what's happening in your current reality. The temporary will change; your current reality will change. When you awaken, when you go through these various stages of awakening, you will leave the pain behind, you will leave the struggle behind. Most of the pain and most of the struggle is from this first stage that people fall into. We all go through it. Most people stay in it forever. They stay in it until they die.

There Is Another Way

It takes most people something like this program to awaken them to teach them that there's another way to live their lives. I know that maybe you're thinking about paying your bills. I know that maybe you're thinking, "How will I pay the rent next month?" I know that maybe you're thinking about your health or somebody who's close to you who has health problems. There is another way to go through all of this. There is another way to resolve these problems. The good news is that I'm delivering this to you personally in *The Awakening Course*.

Well, you might be curious about what my life was like on the streets, and I've never really talked about it in depth. In fact, I never even owned it for the longest time, meaning that, yes, it did happen; yes, I did live on the streets in Dallas, and it was probably around 1976, 1977, 1978, somewhere in there. For the longest time,

I pushed it out of my mind. For the longest time, it never happened in my awareness. But as life went on and people asked me about my history, I'd begin to talk about it, and I found that, though it was uncomfortable for me, it was inspiring for them. So I'll take a moment and touch on that.

I had saved my money and given it all to a company that promised to get work for me overseas. We were building oil and gas pipelines in other countries, in Alaska, places like that, and I had given my money to a company that would make resumes and send out letters, company that promised to get me work. So, I was in Dallas; I had turned over virtually everything I had but some pocket change so I could eat until the job came in, and that company went out of business. It went bankrupt. When I went to find the owner, he had committed suicide, and I was left with no resources. I had gone to Dallas with nothing. I had surrendered all the money I had. I did not have a job. I did not have a car. I did not know anybody. I was in a very rinky-dink apartment in a dangerous area, and I ended up with nothing, sleeping on the steps of a post office. If you've ever seen the movie, *Pursuit of Happyness* with Will Smith, it describes a character who is well-meaning and hardworking, but who makes a few mistakes and, very quickly, is sleeping in a church, sleeping in a toilet stall, sleeping in a bus station. I was doing all of that. I remember sleeping on the steps of the post office because I had a post office box, as I remember, and I kept hoping that a check would come in for something that I had written.

I don't remember everything about that time, because it was very dark and very traumatic psychologically. I did manage, somehow, someway, to leave and get to Houston, and honest to God, I don't remember right now how I did it. I could've hitchhiked. I could've managed to get on a bus somehow. I don't really remember, but I left Dallas, and that wound of being homeless in Dallas stayed with me for at least a decade. I would go back a couple of times for one reason or another, always reluctantly, and something bad would happen.

I remember driving there one time, and as soon as I crossed the Dallas city limits on the highway, a cop pulled me over and gave me a ticket. It was almost as though my mind-set had been lodged in that time and place with this negative charge and that I had to do a lot of cleaning out mentally and becoming more aware, and, as I did, it's no longer a concern. I can go back to Dallas with no problem. I can talk about it as I am with you right now.

It's Only a Story, After All

But the experience was one that, in many ways, made me stronger; in many ways, it has given me a story that has inspired maybe thousands of people. It's possibly inspiring you right now. I would not want to do it again, but I am grateful that I went through it and survived. In many ways, it was a very horrible time. Again, it's part of my makeup and part of my history and part of my past.

In the movie, *The Secret,* there's a scene where all of the different teachers are asked what their life was like: One was in a street gang; I say, "I was homeless"; somebody else had a different hard-luck story; and the next person had yet another tale to tell. Then they cut to Jack Canfield, one of my favorite people in the world, who says, "That's all? So what? We all have a story of some sort. You have a story. I have a story." Part of mine was that I was, indeed, homeless at one point, but I also transcended it.

I'm also in a very different place today. When I look at my life at 30 years ago, being homeless, and today, having a car collection and a country estate and a luxury lifestyle and being a movie star with the movies I'm in and a best-selling author, part of my brain just goes bonkers because it's trying to absorb, "How did *that* person become *this* person?" And that person, the homeless one, became this luxurious one because of an awakening. That's why this material is so important, and that's why I want to share it with you. What

I've learned is practical, spiritual, inspiring, financially rewarding, romantically rewarding, and rewarding in just about every way that you can name. The transformation has been deep and permanent, but it did start with a little blip on the radar where I was homeless at one point.

Well, don't think for a minute that you have to become homeless in order to become awakened. You start wherever you are. Part of what I'm saying here is that you have your own story and that each of us has some past experience that we're growing from, we're growing through, and we're awakening from. You don't have to backpedal; you don't have to become homeless; you don't have to go into debt; you don't have to go into poverty. If you've already experienced all of that, that's all part of your experience. That's simply it. You will transcend it. You will awaken from it. But I'm not asking you in any way, shape, or form to go backward. I'm asking you to go forward, and to go forward through these stages of awakening. That's what I'm taking you through in this material.

Now, I have no idea whether you've already read my earlier books or whether you've heard my audios or seen my DVDs or movies. I have no idea. But what I want you to know is that I'm going to cover the basics and go beyond them. If, for example, you are a fan of my work and you've listened to *The Missing Secret* and you've read *The Attractor Factor* and you've seen the movie *The Secret* (and on and on), it doesn't matter, because what I'm going to be saying in *The Awakening Course* is something I've never, ever talked about before. Again, I'm going to take you from Ground Zero. I'm going to walk you through the basics of awakening. I'm going to describe the four stages of awakening, and the fourth stage of awakening is something I've never talked about before for a very good reason—I didn't know about it.

I have been sharing my own life journey with everybody through my books, my audios, my courses, my movie appearances; I mean, it's still happening. As I grow, as I evolve, as I awaken, as I become more conscious, as I transcend the problems in my own life, I go out and share that with the world, and I'm sharing it as a service to you. If you already know my work, great; if you don't, that's fine, too. Because I'm going to cover all of the basics that are in my materials, but we're also going to go beyond that, so fasten your seatbelt—we're going to have a great time.

It's All Good When You Look Deeper

Why am I doing this now? Why here? Why now? Why is all of this happening right now?

When you look around in the world (especially if you pay attention to the media, which I do *not* recommend), you're probably already thinking, "Oh, Lord. Look what's happening here. There are earth changes going on. There are predictions of doom and gloom." And maybe you're looking at your own life and you're shaky and you're wondering, "How am I going to pay my bills? How am I going to take care of my family? Is my job stable? What's going to happen next? Are we going to run out of gas? Are we going to run out of oil? Are we going to run out of climate control? I mean, just what is happening here?"

I'm going to say something fairly shocking. I'm going to say that it's all happening for the highest good of all concerned. That, actually, these challenges are causing us to look deeply within ourselves to come up with creative solutions, to awaken from the very thing that caused the problems, to transcend everything, and to create a better world, a better place, a better life.

At first glance, it might seem like that's not what's happening and that it doesn't seem possible, but here's just one example: Paul Zane Pilzer, who was an economic adviser to several different presidents, pointed out that in the 1970s, when we went through the oil and gas crisis and it really looked like we would run out of oil and gas and there were long lines at gas stations, the "crisis" (and I intentionally use quotation marks) was actually a stimulus, because engineers invented new ways of digging deeper to find more oil and gas, so we were able to supply ourselves for decades more. (I grew up during that period and remember that people could only buy gas on certain days if their license plate was an odd or an even number. They were very unusual times.) So, what looked like an unsolvable problem was actually a challenge that called for a creative solution.

Well, the same thing is going on in your life right now. It's a positive stimulus if you are sitting there wondering, "How am I going to pay the bills? How am I going to take care of my health and my family? What's going to happen to my job?" It's a good thing. It's making you look in a new direction. It's making you look within yourself. It's making you think more creatively. And it's making you more open. Perhaps if you weren't feeling what you're feeling right now, you never would have invested in *The Awakening Course,* so you never would have been brought here. You might have happily and maybe mindlessly just gone about your merry way and never had an opportunity to grow, never had an opportunity to awaken, so I see that what's going on is actually good.

Yes, it may be uncomfortable, but uncomfortable doesn't mean bad. Uncomfortable simply means you're doing something you haven't done before, so it feels like putting on a new pair of shoes. Very often, you get blisters, even though a new pair of shoes is something good for you; however, your skin will heal, it will actually toughen, you will grow from it, and you'll be walking around with new shoes in a new life, feeling much more optimistic and abundant and looking forward to the future. That's the promise of what looks like a challenge.

Stop Struggling—There's an Easier Way

Well, if you look at your life, most likely you've been working a little too hard, and that's because you have been—and maybe I'm making a new word here—"efforting" through your life, meaning that you've been struggling through your life, that you've been fighting through your life. I actually remember that, in high school and college, I admired a lot of the authors like Jack London and Ernest Hemingway, because it was one man against the world; I admired that because that's how I felt. It was just Joe Vitale against planet Earth, which is how most of us lead our lives. We're coming from a particular mind-set that says, if anything's going to get done, I'm going to have to work at it and struggle at it, and I'm going to have to deprive myself of certain things, and I'm going to have to just really fight my way through life. Well, that's a belief that creates the very reality that the belief is fueling. In other words, if you *believe* that you have to struggle to get anywhere, you will create struggle to get anywhere. If you *believe* that you have to suffer to get anywhere, you will suffer to get anywhere.

Let me give you a very clearheaded example. I told you about being homeless at one point. What awakened me to how I created that in my own life was the insight that I was modeling my life after authors who were self-destructive. Jack London allegedly committed suicide. Ernest Hemingway committed suicide. I admired these authors to the extent that I thought I had to lead the same kind of life as them because that was the curriculum. So I was going down a very self-destructive path. I was fighting with life. I was making sure that I was unhappy. I was making sure that I was struggling. I was making sure that I was miserable. I finally realized I was doing that because of a belief—the belief that, in order for me to be a successful author, which was my goal, I had to suffer like they did. I was an alcoholic; I was suicidal; I was melancholy. I was going down the same road those people had gone, until one day I awakened to the idea that

I could model their writing styles, but I didn't necessarily have to model their lifestyle. When I realized *that*, I began to find authors who were happy and productive and prosperous. When I found *that*, I began to create a new reality for myself. So, what I'm suggesting— and, again, it may be hard to understand when you first hear this—is the idea that you are struggling needlessly. You have been struggling in the past. It has served you well. You've learned. You've grown. You've gotten stronger from doing that. But at this point, you can let that go. I'm going to show you an easier way. I'm going to show you the escalator. I'm going to show you how to awaken from what has created the struggle in the past so that you can have the wealth, the success, the romance, the abundance, all of what you want without the struggle. You won't have to be "efforting" your life. You can be flowing your life.

You might be wondering where these beliefs are within you. They're not typically in your conscious mind. They're in your unconscious mind.

The Missing Secret

In a program called *The Missing Secret,* I said that the missing secret is the idea that you have to get clear of the beliefs within your own mind before you start to see the results in the outer world. What I'm very excited about is that in this book I'm going to show you how to find those limiting beliefs and change those limiting beliefs. Perhaps you are concerned that, "Oh, I've been creating this struggle in my life, but I don't know why I'm creating it, because I'm not a writer; I wasn't modeling myself after Ernest Hemingway or Jack London like you were, but you were doing something." There is a belief that's active in your mind that is creating the reality you have. I'm going to help you find that belief, clear that belief, so you are free of that belief, and the really exciting thing about all of this is, once you're free of that belief, you change the entire world—because the belief wasn't active only *within* you. Because it was active within you, it extended into the universe itself, and the universe rearranged itself to make that belief true.

Again, when you first hear all of this, it might seem a little bizarre, but stick with me. By reading and applying *The Awakening Course,* you will get to the understanding that you are creating your own reality, and we're actually going to go past even that in the fourth stage of awakening. But, for now, don't worry about any of this. If you have been struggling, that's fine because the good news is, the struggle is over.

You Can "Take It to the Bank"

Now, I'm also excited to tell you that I'm going to be giving you a lot of practical tools, exercises, even a couple of meditations. All of this is to help make your life easier. All of this is to help clear those beliefs that might be holding you back a little bit. All of this is to help you awaken. I'm a very practical, savvy, level-headed fellow. I am an entrepreneur. I want to see results. I want to see results in your life. So this isn't some sort of feel-good program, some kind of wifty mumbo jumbo. This is a very much a "take-it-to-the-bank" program. I want you to try these techniques, try the meditations, listen to what I have to say about beliefs. Go through the four steps in *The Awakening Course* and then see where you are, because where you are now is not where you're going to be at the end of this program. Where you are now is temporary. Where you're going is eternal. Stick with me.

Fear Will Only Stop You if You Let It

The number one thing you're going to have to watch for as you go through this program (and, actually, going through life itself) is the whole element of fear. Fear is everywhere. As I look around, I notice that it seems like the whole planet is up in arms and everybody's afraid of everything and everybody. And, if you listen to the media (which, again, I do *not* recommend), it always focuses on the fear and gives you reasons to be afraid. However, if you don't pay attention to it, you don't have those reasons, which is pretty interesting. Fear will stop you if you let it.

I'm not asking you to hold your breath and stand in front of a train or a bus or a car, but I am asking you to take a moment to see if you are being fearful of simple change. A lot of people don't want to change because they are comfortable where they are. They look around, and where they are right now feels like it's okay. It's comfortable. I might be in debt, I might not like my job, I might be in a relationship I don't care for, and I might have a bad back, but it's okay—it's the known. Well, it may be time for you to get a little uncomfortable and to awaken from all of that so you can have more. If you sit there in fear saying, "I want to stay where I am," you will stay where you are, so again, there's a difference between leaving your comfort zone and actually going into the fear mode. Fear is going to stop you. Fear is what stops most people from taking action. I've found in my career that there's the fear of failure and the fear of success, and some people have both of them.

Transcend Your Fear

What I'm talking about is transcending fear. What I'm talking about is inviting you to dare something worthy in your life by focusing on what you want, and, as you focus on what you want, you might be called to do a few things you've never done before, but it doesn't mean that you should be afraid of them. The uneasy feeling that you have is *only* because you're doing something new. It's not a signal to stop. It's not a signal to fall into fear. It is a sign that you are doing something new and that you should just be alert as you go ahead and do it. That's what I'm asking you to do in this program—as one famous book says, I'm asking you to "feel the fear and do it anyway." Feel the discomfort and do it anyway. Stick with me, because I promise an awakening, and it all begins here, now, today.

Inventory Your Fears

List the things that you're afraid of. Just go ahead and list anything and everything. There's something therapeutic about just writing them down. When you get them out of your system, in many ways they dissolve, because you look at them on paper and you realize, "Oh, that's not so scary after all." Taking inventory of the fears is a way of cleaning house. So empty your mind of your concerns, write down any and all fears. This is not something you have to show me. You don't have to show it to anybody. It's for your eyes only, so it's a very safe exercise. Write down all of your fears and just take a deep breath as you're doing it. Just let them go. You might even look at each one of the fears and ask yourself, "Do I really fear that?" It's okay to say yes and it's okay to say no, but breathe through it as you are listing them because you may find that a lot of them dissolve simply by taking the inventory of them. Go ahead, pause and do that now.

I mentioned earlier about the power of the unconscious mind, so when you start to write down your fears, you may not at first have many. But because you focused on this and you've called them from your mind, they'll start bubbling up from your unconscious. That's actually a good thing. Don't be afraid of that. Just start writing down your fears. As you write down one fear, another one may surface. As you write down that one, another may surface. There may be tangential fears to any of the ones you've listed.

You might even take a breather after you've written down as many as you can think of, whether it's 5 or 50. Take a deep breath, wait, and say, "Is there anything else I'm afraid of?" Go ahead and write down whatever comes up. Again, trust yourself, trust your unconscious mind. It'll bubble up as it feels safe to do so, so just make a nice, safe place for you to list your fears, because we're going to let them all go.

Mine Your Fear for Buried Treasure

I've created a Miracles Coaching program to help people awaken, to help them achieve their dreams, and to help them overcome their fears. But let me tell you a story, a true story, about what happened to me at one point. A long time ago, I wrote a book called *Spiritual Marketing*. And, in many ways, this was a dangerous booklet. It was dangerous because I represented a lot of conservative companies: American Marketing Association had published one of my books; American Management Association had published another of my books; Nightingale-Conant had published one of my audio programs. These companies were very conservative, and I wondered what in the world they'd think of me if I came out with *Spiritual Marketing*, which was a metaphysical, otherworldly kind of approach to doing business. So I just published the book as a little pamphlet, which I would hand out here and there, in addition to giving it to my sister, for whom I wrote it. I was trying to help her get through her fears and become more aware and awake and to achieve some of her dreams.

I gave one to Bob Proctor at one of his "Science of Getting Rich" workshops. It was in Denver, probably around 1999. I gave it to him as a gift. I never expected him to tell anybody about it, but he stood on stage in front of 250 people and told them that there was a celebrity in the room, and as he read off all the titles, I knew he was talking about me. I stood up and took a bow. Then he said, "And Joe has written a new book, an unpublished book, and a book everybody is going to want. It's called *Spiritual Marketing*." Well, I was a nervous wreck thinking, "Oh, they're going to hang me at this point. They're going to take me out and torch me." But instead, 250 people rushed me, all of whom wanted the book. I was awash in 160 business cards from these people. There was a publisher among them who said he wanted to publish the book. And I said, "Why? You haven't even seen the book." He said, "Well, you're obviously an author. You've been published before. You must know how to write. Bob Proctor has read the book and he likes it." He said, "I'll publish it sight unseen."

Well, the short story is that I was terrified of letting that book go out, but because I was pushed a little bit by Bob Proctor in 1999 or thereabouts, that book became a best seller. It was reincarnated into my book, *The Attractor Factor.* I rewrote it, expanded it, and retitled it. A big publisher picked it up. Because of *The Attractor Factor,* I ended up in the movie *The Secret.* Rhonda Byrne, who was the creator of *The Secret,* called me after reading *The Attractor Factor,* said she had this idea for a movie, and asked if I would be interested in a role in it if she got the money together and the script and all of that. Well, I didn't know her from anybody else. I didn't know if she'd actually do this or not, but she did. Of course, the rest is history because *The Secret* has been an epidemic. It has just awakened the planet on at least a Stage Two level, and it's put me on *Larry King* twice and *Donny Deutsch.* It also paved the way for my appearance in four other movies and, of course, in the book version of *The Secret.* It's led to other book deals for me. I could go on and on. There was a whole domino effect from the release of *Spiritual Marketing,* but I was afraid. I was afraid to release it. Somebody had to encourage me . . . and I'm a great believer in encouraging people. That's something I want to talk about with you, because I'm here to encourage you to go for your dream. I'm here to encourage you to dare something worthy. I'm here to encourage you to awaken. Bob Proctor encouraged me and embarrassed me in front of 250 people, but I learned that, very often, when you face your fears, your wealth, your success, your romance—the things, the materials, that you're actually looking for—are right behind what you fear. This is why it's so important to face your fears. Behind them is treasure.

Money Is Good

One of the things I'm excited about sharing with you in this program is the idea that abundance is actually okay. That money is actually good. I have learned that a lot of people push money away. They actually say they want money, but internally, unconsciously, they're afraid of it. I'm going to be exploring that with you in *The Awakening Course*. I'm going to be helping you with that, because a lot of people will consciously say, "I want a new job," "I want my book published," "I want my business to succeed," "I want to have a lot of money in the bank," "I want to be debt-free," "I want to be financially free," but unconsciously, what do you think they're saying? "Money is bad. Money is evil. I don't deserve money. Rich people are snobs. Taxes will consume all my money." All of these are beliefs and all of these are fears. On a top-level conscious mind, they're saying, "I want money." Below the surface, in the unconscious mind, which is the more powerful operating system, they're saying, "I don't want money because I'm afraid of it," and they're pushing it away. I've learned that money is good. I've learned that money can actually serve me. It's just a tool that has no energy in and of itself. We all put energy into acquiring it. You do it. I do it. But money, in and of itself, is pure. It's paper, it's coin, it's whatever value we say it has, but we can use it to accomplish miracles.

Contribute a Happy, Healthy, Wealthy Person to the World

I've told people that if they really want to make a difference in the world, if they want the world to be a happier, healthier, wealthier place, then contribute one happy, healthy, wealthy person to it—you.

Spiritual Marketing

Now, I'm known as a spiritual marketer, and, as I mentioned, I wrote a little booklet called *Spiritual Marketing*, which became *The Attractor Factor,* and I believe that the spiritual and material are two sides of the same coin. They're not opposites at all. You don't dismiss either one of them. You need both of them to have an awakened life. You need the spirituality and you need the financial part of it in order to walk through this world. You need the essence, your spirit, within your body, but you also need your body in order to get around in this world that we have today. It's not exclusively one or the other: Both are valued; both are needed; and both are integrated into one unit.

I also talk about things like marketing, yet I won't be teaching you marketing in this course; other programs that I have address that. This book is about awakening, awakening to the life that you would love to have on all levels. But the thing I want to point out is that when I talk to people about marketing, I hear that they often have a negative or bad idea about marketing. That's the old-school approach, where you try to manipulate people to get money from them. I do not believe in that at all. I believe that marketing is sharing your love for your product or service with the people who will most welcome hearing about it. I'm going to say that again because I think that is the profound new definition of marketing as I know it and want it to be in the world: *Marketing is sharing your love for your product or service with the people who most want to hear about it, and who will most welcome it when they do hear about it.*

Love Is the Essence

When I talk about *The Awakening Course,* for example, I'm doing it out of my passion. I'm doing it out of my caring for you. I am doing it out of my love. If this reaches you, and apparently it already has, and you've invested in this book, then you realize that you're welcoming it. So I've connected to you on a heart level. My heart has reached out to you, and you've invested in this book you're now reading. This is all based in love. Love is what I think marketing, money, life, abundance, romance, and spirituality are all about. Love is the essence for all of this. Love is the essence of *The Awakening Course*. As we go through this together, that will become very, very clear.

Practical Benefits

Okay. Let's summarize what we've been talking about, and let me go over the benefits you're going to be getting from this program.

For one thing, you're going to get out of debt, and that means paying off your credit cards, taking care of your house payments, taking care of your car payments, or anything else that might be holding you in debt right now. It might seem impossible to you right now, but that's based on your current mind-set. As you go through these four stages of awakening, you will see how you can actually pay off your debt. You can see how you can become financially free, and "financially free" actually means free of worries about money, wealth, and finances. Again, this might seem impossible. Stay with me. And if you're okay right now with money, if you already have plenty of it, if you are financially free, if you're debt-free, if you're doing just great with finances, you may not be doing so great in other areas. For example, you might have some issues with romance, with relationships, with the love of your life, maybe even loving yourself. All of this is going to be addressed in this book. You might be dealing with a health issue. There might be somebody in your life who is dealing with a health issue. You might be concerned about aging. You might be concerned about losing weight or gaining weight. We're going to be talking about all of that.

As a side note, I lost 80-odd pounds and entered seven fitness contests—this after a lifetime of childhood and adult obesity. If I can do it, you can do it, and so can anybody else involved.

The Key *Is* Happiness

If you're also trying to find happiness, this is a key ingredient in the whole awakening program. Finding happiness, as you're going to find out, is a key to achieving everything you want, and I'm going to explain that, in detail, and show you ways to become happy now. You'll find out that you can be happy no matter what's going on in your life, that you don't have to change the people around you or your job or the things around you in order to find happiness or to be happy now. And don't beat yourself up for wanting worldly things. There's nothing wrong with cars and houses and toys and making a difference in your own personal life. Those are all fun. Those are all worth going for, and, as you go through the stages of awareness and awakening, you'll get to a place where you will automatically, naturally, and lovingly want to make a difference in the world, too. That doesn't mean you have to become another Gandhi. It doesn't mean that you have to starve. It doesn't mean that you have to do anything that's unappealing to you, but there will be something that will come from your heart that will be a natural extension of who you are.

Four Stages of Awareness

As we go through this program, I'll talk about how that has worked in my own life. I still like cars, but I also still want to make a difference in people's lives. For example, I'd like to resolve homelessness, and I've started a movement to end that forever. Wanting cars, fancy rings, or anything else is totally fine—I'll also be helping you go up the four levels of awareness. Again, I've never talked about the fourth level, so even if you are familiar with me and my work, this is going to be new. This is brand new. And if you aren't familiar with my work, remember, I'm going to take you from kindergarten to first grade and on through to graduate school, on through to the different levels, ending with the fourth level. We will be going through these stages of enlightenment, these stages of awareness, as we go through this book.

Endless Possibilities

Keep in mind that you may want something bigger than what some people consider to be selfish goals. You might actually want world peace; you might actually try to make a difference in the world in some particular area or some particular country. The principles I'm going to be teaching you here are applicable there as well. You can actually achieve virtually anything that you can imagine with this program. I'm going to walk you through all of those steps.

I guess it's worth mentioning right now that this is just you and me. I'm talking to you and, as I'm sitting here and you are sitting there, I'm speaking from my heart. What's coming up from me is partly inspiration, partly divine guidance, partly based on my past education and things that I definitely want to communicate with you, but I don't have a script. I'm ad-libbing this. I'm speaking from my heart to your heart, and that's an essential part of this whole program as well.

To awaken, you want to come from your heart. *Heart, love, happiness*—those are key words, and they'll resurface as you go through this program. So, stay with me as we go through *The Awakening Course*.

Meditation

All of these stages will make a rich difference in your life, beginning right now, because what I'm going to ask you to do next is to actually do a small meditation. Remember when I asked you to make that list of fears? Look at that list and breathe through it. Just look at your fears, one by one, and take in a deep breath. When you take in your breath, hold it for the count of five and look at your little list, then exhale for the count of three, and then take in another breath. Again, just causally breathing, gently relaxing, as you look at your list of fears. As you look at the list and breathe, you notice that you are becoming less fearful. These fears don't have the charge that they originally did. If you still feel a little uncomfortable about the fears that are on the list, that's okay, I'm not asking you to do anything with the fears themselves. You're simply breathing in, holding it for a small count of five, releasing for a short count of three, and breathing in again.

As you cycle through that for a few minutes, you just ease into your day and you ease into the moment and you ease into this place where you are not afraid. You might notice later that if you run into any of these fears, they actually don't have much intimidation to them. They're lighter. They're easier. You are freer with them. You may, in fact, be free of them. Don't overthink this. Don't over-feel this. Simply enjoy the breathing, the taking in of your list, and the letting go. I'll see you in the next chapter as we continue *The Awakening Course*.

Chapter 2

Stage One
Victimhood

The only time there are bumps on the road is when you have inner beliefs that are still limiting you from enjoying them. I was homeless at one point in my life. What happened in me is that I learned the secret. I said that if you're not wealthy and you want to be wealthy, it's probably because of the counterintentions within yourself. You can take all kinds of action, have all kinds of intentions, watch The Secret over and over and over again. Some people watch it two hundred times. Two hundred times! But you won't get a change if you don't take care of the counterintentions.

—Joe Vitale

Confusion before Clarity

Welcome to Stage One in *The Awakening Course*. At this point, you might actually be a little confused, and that's actually okay. I have a friend named Mandy Evans, a delightful soul, who wrote a book called *Emotional Options,* then a second book called *Travelling Free*. She once said, "Confusion is that wonderful state of mind right before clarity." I've always loved that, because I've been confused many times in my life, but I've noticed that it always pops, the clouds clear, the sun comes out, and suddenly I have a new awareness. Again, that's what we're talking about here. If you're confused right now, it's perfectly fine and you're right on schedule. In fact, you may become confused a few more times throughout this program. So stay with me and enjoy the process.

Learn to Recognize the Victim Mind-Set

We're going to be talking about the very first stage of awakening. In many ways, the very first stage isn't about awakening at all, because when you're born, you have the mind-set of a victim. You don't have that as a label on your forehead, and you probably don't think that at all. But we're programmed from birth on to give in to outer authority. It begins shortly after birth, when our parents start showing us how the world works. Now, if you understand that we are in a belief-generated world, that your beliefs create your reality, you understand that your parents have beliefs that are creating their reality. Those parents are downloading their beliefs directly into your experience. When you're born, you're unconscious. You're not a blank slate, but you are close to a blank slate. You are absorbing what your parents are saying, you are watching what they're doing, and you are making conclusions. You're drawing decisions from everything that they're doing.

For example, if they think having money is hard to achieve, if they think money is bad, if they dwell on health problems in their lives, very likely you have taken on those attitudes as well. There's a whole lot of programming, if you will, that comes from your parents, but it doesn't stop there. Your parents send you to school. In school, you're taught how the world works. Yet the school system doesn't necessarily teach how to awaken. It teaches how to survive. And from a survival standpoint, it does a fair job, not an immaculate job in any way, shape, or form, but school is also programming you about lack and limitation. It's programming you about the lack of abundance in the world, that there's actually scarcity in the world. Again, you're not consciously thinking about any of this.

Religion does the same thing. Your parents have beliefs about the universe, about God, about the Divine. You absorb that, most likely without questioning it. I'm not saying this is good, bad, or indifferent; I'm saying that for the longest time you are trained to be at the will of somebody else, whether it's your government, which also does some programming, or whether it's the media, which is also doing a lot of programming. What you're watching on television, what you're watching on the news, what you're seeing these days on the Internet is programming you on a different level. All of this, whether it's coming from your parents, from the school, from the government, from religion, from the media, is programming you to be under the thumb of somebody else.

The First Stage: It's All About Being a Victim

This first stage is all about being a victim. Most people will sadly go to their death feeling like they have been victims. They'll work within that victim mentality to try to make a difference in their life. For example, I mentioned earlier that I was homeless at one point. I wanted to get work. Well, I did the standard things that a victim mentality does. I applied for jobs. When I had a job, I did the standard thing a victim mentality does—I tried to get a different job. I also did things like writing resumes for different kinds of people. And I saw that the people who came in, even top-level CEOs and executives, had this mentality that they were victims, too, and that they were looking for jobs that paid about the same as they were already receiving. Maybe they wanted a little more money, maybe they wanted a few more benefits, maybe they wanted to work in a different environment doing something a little different. But they were giving their power to someone else, and they also had a sense that they didn't deserve more than they were already getting. All of this was coming from this victim mind-set. This is the first stage that you need to awaken from.

Only Victims Blame and Complain

You may not know that you're in a vicious cycle of recrimination; maybe you do. I had to go through a long period. I remember when I was growing up, I blamed God, I blamed my parents, I blamed the school system, I blamed everybody for what I was going through, and I was very unhappy. I blamed them because I didn't want to take responsibility, and I didn't know how to take responsibility. That was not a concept in my mind. I was coming from being a victim without knowing I was a victim. When I said earlier that I admired authors like Jack London and Earnest Hemmingway, it was because they were fighting the system; they were fighting nature; they were fighting the elements. And, according to their fictional writings, they were winning. I found that I was trying to do that, and I felt like I was losing. I wasn't getting ahead in the world, and this made me unhappy; this made me very much in the mind-set of struggle. I was doing that "efforting" we were talking about earlier.

All of this was because I was a victim and I didn't know it. Henry David Thoreau said, "The mass of men lead lives of quiet desperation." Well, I was quietly, and sometimes noisily, desperate myself. If you look around, you've probably heard yourself complain about the system, about the government, about the president, about the terrorists, about anything else that's going on in the world. It could be your neighbors, your family, your friends—and doesn't it sound like you're being a victim? What we're talking about in this first stage is awakening to the fact that you have been thinking like a victim. As soon as you awaken to that thought, you can begin to work within it. Meaning that you're still feeling like a victim, but you've awakened to this simple idea: "Since I've been a victim, maybe if I do a few things differently, I can transcend this first stage." Most people, again, are born into this and never awaken from it, so they can't go to Stage Two, they can't go to Stage Three, they can't go to Stage Four, because they haven't awakened to being a victim in Stage One.

If you're confused about this, don't worry about it. It will become clear as we keep moving forward. I also want you to not dismiss anything. I want you to digest everything. These ideas may seem foreign to you because no one else has spoken to you this directly (from my heart to your heart) in this particular manner, about this material.

Again, digest this; don't dismiss it. Stay with me on this track; let's keep going together and find out how the world really works.

Seven Keys to Breaking Out of the Victim Pattern

To help you understand the victim mentality and how to break from it (actually to become aware of it and begin to leap into the next stage), let me talk about the seven key points. These seven key principles can help you awaken to the first stage and begin to go into the second stage of awakening. I want to go through these seven key points with you right now. And if you're a little confused as you hear them, smile and realize that, as we go along our way, it will all become clear.

1. Take 100 Percent Responsibility

You are totally responsible for your experiences in your life. You were not to blame for them; it's not your fault; but it is your responsibility.

2. Unconscious Absorption

The second is, you are absorbing beliefs from the culture itself. It's unconscious. This goes back to what I said before: When you're born, you start receiving and downloading information and beliefs about how to live, about how the world works. You're not thinking about this; this is all unconscious.

3. You Are More Powerful than You Know

The third principle is, you are not ruler of the earth. You're not God. But you have more power than you ever realized. Again, that might feel inspiring or maybe intimidating, depending on how you look at it while you're still in the first stage of victim mentality, but just sit with this for a while and see how it feels.

4. *Become Aware of Your Thoughts*

The fourth is, you can change your thoughts, but you need to become aware of them to do so. This is pretty interesting, because a lot of people aren't aware that they're having thoughts. They *are* their thoughts. In the first stage of being a victim, the thinking is going on, but the thinking is you. You are identified with it; you are not separate from it. Stay with me on this. Right now, you're thinking about this program, but if you pause for a moment, you might realize that you are watching yourself thinking about this program. There is thinking, and then there's awareness of thinking. So you are thinking about this program, but if you don't detach just one little element from it, you'll feel like you are the thinking. In order to change your thoughts, you must become aware that you are separate from your thoughts. This is a very profound, very powerful, very important first step to understanding how to leave the victim mentality and start to enter Stage Two.

5. *You Are Limitless*

The next step is to understand that you can do the impossible. You don't know your limits. I love this one, too, because a lot of people will say, "Oh, there are certainly things that are impossible; there are certainly limits." Well, when you're in the victim mentality, you feel as though that's the case. But if you start looking at old history, if you start looking at old science, and you see the amazing breakthroughs that are going on right now, you start to realize that there really aren't any limits, and there really isn't anything that's impossible. When we talk about what's possible today, it's based on our understanding of what science and physics currently tell us is possible and impossible. But science and physics keep changing as we learn more about ourselves.

So, just for the moment, entertain the idea that you can do the impossible, that you don't know your limits, and that is very true. You do not know your limits. You have not tried everything. You may not have tried much of anything. When you do, you'll find out what your limits are. And when you change your beliefs, you'll find that there aren't any limits. There are only mental constraints.

6. Emotion Is the Fuel

The sixth point is this: Whatever image you add emotion to will tend to manifest. And this is something that's powerful. Have you ever noticed in your life that what you truly love or what you truly hate seems to show up all around you? It's because you've had an image, and you've added intense feeling to it. I'll explain this a little more as we go through this course. For now, I just want you to entertain the idea that what you visualize in your mind with feeling, with intense feeling, especially if it's love or hate, will tend to be attracted into your awareness, into your life experience.

7. Let Go

Finally, number seven, you can have miracles when you let go of attachment and need. This is very profound, and I'm going to say something that will be very shocking at first, but this is the honest-to-God truth. You can have whatever you want, as long as you don't need it.

This will make more sense later. But it's the idea that when you are attached to something, when you are addicted to something, when you need something to happen, you actually send off an energy that repels it. It doesn't come into your life experience. When you are more playful about what you would like to have, you send off this energy of love, this energy of detachment, and just the energy of simple wanting. Chances are that what you wish will rapidly come into your life simply because you're playful about it.

Everybody's Doing It

Okay, as you read about those seven principles that are going to help you leave the first stage of awakening and go into the second stage, maybe you had some thoughts about them, maybe you had some beliefs about them. Maybe you didn't understand them. How did you feel? What I'm getting at is that the experience of victimhood can be a little sneaky. It can be going on below your awareness, and you have to pay attention to what you're saying to yourself. You could be saying, "Oh, that Dr. Joe Vitale doesn't make any sense at all."

Say, for example, you had a car accident. Who would you blame? If you read the newspapers and you see that something is going on, be it the oil crisis or a terrorist alert, who do you blame? Do you look within yourself, or do you say something like, "It's the president's fault," "It's the government's fault," "It's the fault of the political parties fault"? If you have a problem at work, who do you blame? Do you say it's because of the boss? Do you say it's because of a particular supervisor? Do you say it's because of the weather? Usually, people who are coming from a victimhood mentality are blaming everybody else. They are pointing their fingers all around them.

So the first thing I want you to be aware of is that we all do it. I do it, and you are probably doing it right now. You probably have been doing it all along; you probably did it sometime today or yesterday. All I'm asking you to do right now is to be aware of it. That's the whole point of this book. That's why it's called *The Awakening Course*. As you become aware, you can become awake.

A Sense of Freedom

As I went through those seven principles, maybe you were wrestling with them; maybe you weren't. But you were probably thinking about them. I want you to look at the idea that you are not your thoughts.

Now, if this is something you have been doing for a long time, just stay with me, because we are going to go to the advanced stuff pretty soon. So, you've been reading through these seven principles, and you have been thinking about them. Did you realize you were thinking about them? Let me ask it differently. Right now, as I'm asking this question, thoughts are going through your mind. Are you shaking your head, wondering what I'm talking about, or are you taking a deep breath and realizing, "Thoughts are going through my mind, but I'm not my thoughts." They're just kind of going through like clouds going through the sky. Thoughts are on the canvas of awareness. You are not that thought. You are not the next thought. You can watch those thoughts; you can be detached from those thoughts. And, as you are, there is a sense of freedom. There is a beginning of an opening to a new state of awareness.

For now, just watch your thoughts, and in fact, take a moment and breathe through those, because this is a very powerful turning point in your life. It's easy to say you're a victim. It's easy to point fingers at other people. It's easy to dismiss the seven principles I've just introduced. However, I'm asking you to trust me. I've been through this. I've gone through all four stages of awakening. And I'm helping you through this first one.

When I told you that I was homeless at one point and that I couldn't go back to Dallas, it's because I had that victimhood mentality for the longest time. It manifested itself over and over again whenever I went back to Dallas. I'm suggesting that, if you've done work on yourself from other books or audio programs of one sort or another, you actually might have a little bit of victim mentality still in you in some areas. Maybe you're doing fine with your romance, but maybe you're not doing so fine with your health. Well, who are you blaming for that? If you're not doing so well with your finances, who are you blaming for that? I had to go back to Dallas two or three times, and I actually had to see a "miracles coach" to help relieve me of the beliefs that were still active within me.

As we go through this program, I'm going to give you exercises, meditations, and techniques to help relieve you of those beliefs, too, so that you can be free, so that you're no longer a victim, so that every area of your life is a joyous one. That's the promise of *The Awakening Course,* and that's the promise of beginning by entertaining the ideas of these seven principles and by paying attention to your thoughts.

It's Not about the Past

Please understand the difference here, because you might have had something happen in your life that you were a victim of. I'm not talking about an experience that happened that's in the past. It's over with. You may find you need to do some healing from it. I'm talking about a mentality. I'm talking about a thought pattern that might attract some of these things that happen to you, a thought pattern that might actually keep you in a circumstance that you don't want to be in anymore, but you're there because you feel like a victim.

Yes, people have heart attacks; they have health problems; they experience crime of one sort or another. People do have victim experiences. That's not what I'm referring to here (although that may be part of it, especially if it's a recurring pattern in your life). I'm talking about the mind-set that always says, "You are not going to win." Within that mind-set, you might make some effort. You might purchase a goal-setting book. You might go to a therapist. You might fill out forms to apply for a new job, or answer ads, or write a new resume. But you're still working within the framework of this first stage of awakening. You're still coming from this victim mentality, and what you want to do is realize that the past does not equal the future. What happened in the past does not have to reoccur. What you want to have in your life can come into your life once you've cleaned up your thinking about what's going on in your life.

A New Sense of Power

Again, taking a deep breath, pay attention to your beliefs, pay attention to your thinking, and start to be aware that maybe, just maybe, you have blamed the world for everything that's gone on. And maybe, just maybe, you have more power than you ever thought possible. As you reflect on the seven principles that I gave you earlier, go back and read them again; as you start to take them in, you'll probably begin to feel a new sense of power. And as you feel this new sense of power, that will take you from being a victim into the second stage, which I'm excited about taking you to. I know from being in the victim mentality, and I stayed in it for the longest time, that it's not a very pleasant place to be. You don't even know how wonderful life can be, because you feel like you are under a dark cloud all the time. As you pay attention to your thoughts and start to entertain the idea that you can have more than you ever imagined, as you start to leave the blaming mentality, and as you start to take on the responsibility mentality, you start to awaken in this first stage.

Even Victims Have Choice

Keep in mind that when something happens to you, and you're coming from the victim mentality, you still have choice. Some people who have the victim mentality don't know that they have choice. But some do, and they make a different choice. In other words, two people can come from the same family and have very similar experiences of abuse, yet one will carry that abuse and that judgment and that pain and that trauma forever, while the other one might turn it into something good. The other one might become a healer who writes books about people who have gone through similar abuse, thus using the experience to transform others. You always have a choice. When something happens to you, you can look at it as profoundly negative, or you can look at it as a wonderful opportunity. That goes for just about everything that happens. Even within the victim mentality, you have a choice about how you're going to act and what it means to you.

Mandy Evans is someone I mentioned earlier. She wrote *Emotional Options* and *Travelling Free*. In the latter, she addresses the idea of being a victim. She has people go back to the past and look at whatever happened to them, and she points out that it's not what happens to you that matters, it's what you determine it means. This is very important, because if you look at something as a very horrible experience that can never be forgiven or forgotten, you're going to carry that hurt for a very long time. You're going to be very unhappy and probably even attract similar experiences. Certainly, those memories will be there, and they're not very pleasant. But Mandy Evans proposes that if you can look at that same memory, that same experience, and change the meaning of it, perhaps you can find some sort of good in it.

You Don't Have to Wait to Find the Good

There's an author by the name of Kurt Wright. In my book, *The Attractor Factor*, I quote him, and here I'll paraphrase him. He says that you can think back to something that happened to you maybe a year ago, and when it happened, it felt very negative, and you felt like a victim at that point. He goes on to say that, now, at this point, a year later, you have this sense of detachment that allows you to see that maybe it was good for you, and perhaps you can even see the humor in it. Maybe when you tell the story of what happened to you a year ago, you have everybody laughing. Wright says if you are able to have that sense of humor and detachment one year after the event, maybe it was available at the time it happened.

This is profound if you pause and think about it. It means that no matter what has happened to you in your life, no matter what level of victimization you may have felt, you can look at it and say there was some sort of positive benefit in it. When I told you the story about me being homeless and struggling in poverty for a very long time, I pointed out that it actually helped me grow. It actually helped me have a story that is inspiring people, possibly even inspiring you. For that reason alone, it was actually something good. I'm not suggesting you should go back and say that everything that happened to you was good, because I do know that sometimes things happen to you and they have a sting. The sting may still be there. It's okay, I'm sending you love right now as I'm talking to you and you're reading these words. As we go through this, you will awaken from it and go to a whole new level. Einstein said: "The significant problems we have cannot be solved by the same level of thinking with which we created them."

Again, this is all about transcending thinking. This is all about becoming aware of our thinking so we can go through these four stages of awakening. And you have to awaken from the very first one, when you are a victim and don't even know it. One of the first ways to do that is to become aware of your thinking. What are you thinking right now? Who are you blaming right now? Realize that you are actually detached from your thoughts.

Challenge Yourself to Stop Complaining

Let me tell you something fascinating. One of my favorite books in the world is *A Complaint Free World* by Will Bowen. I have since met the author, interviewed him, and I am now on his board of directors to actually start a movement to end complaining on the planet. On one level, this sounds a little preposterous. We all complain, especially victims. Victims are always complaining about everybody else. Well, Will Bowen has issued this challenge. This is a useful technique to use within this first stage. You can carry it into the second stage for sure, and it's a useful technique no matter where you are in your thinking process, your growth process, your awareness process; it helps wherever you are on the stage of life. Bowen issued this challenge: to not complain for 30 days straight. The whole point of this exercise is to become aware.

I love it, because I believe in the power of intention, and I'll be telling you about that later in the book. Bowen says that just before you're going to complain, stop. You hear it in your thoughts; you hear that you're just about to complain about the guy who pulled out in front of you, or your boss, or your significant other. Then something goes on in your brain; the alarm bell rings; you were about to complain about something. And you pause, and you pause, and you turn it into what you want. Instead of stating your complaint, you state your intention.

This is going to be new for you if you've never done this or you haven't read my book, *The Attractor Factor*, or seen the movie, *The Secret*. I will elaborate on this whole subject later. What I want you to do now is to become aware of your thinking. This is very important in this first stage when you're beginning to feel like you're a victim, but you're waking up to the reality that maybe you can actually leave this victimhood behind. Maybe you can have more control in this. And one way to start to feel that power is to pay attention to what you're about to speak. Not to what you're speaking—to what you're *about to* speak. A thought has formed in your head, and you're about to vocalize it, complain, but you hold your tongue. You pause, and you think, "What would I rather have?" For example, when a bill arrives in the mail, instead of stating the complaint, "I don't have enough money for it," you would state the intention, "I want to have enough money to pay this bill and all other bills."

It's Okay to Feel Uncomfortable

This might feel uncomfortable. It's the first time you're doing this kind of thinking and this kind of intention setting. If you've been in the victimhood mentality for quite some time, it will feel like you're trying on a new suit that maybe doesn't quite fit you yet. But this is like learning anything else. As you practice, it will become easier. It's very important in this first stage to pay attention to your thinking.

Change Your Language

I want to give you another tip. When you're thinking, you can learn to play with language, even while you're in this first stage of victim mentality. Where most people say they have a problem, you can begin calling problems "opportunities." This is a shift in mind-set. By playing with the language, you can change phrases that use "I have to," such as "I have to work out," "I have to go to work," I have to do this," to the more positive "I get to work out. I get to go to work. I get to go on this particular date." *I get to* [do whatever it was you were about to say] is more affirmative, whereas *I have to* has more of a complaint ring to it. It has more of a negative ring to it. It has more of a victim ring to it. By changing your language, you are actually taking control of your own reality. Instead of saying there is a "setback," you say there is a "challenge." Instead of saying, "I have an enemy," you say, "I actually have a friend." Instead of saying there is a tormentor in your life, you say, "There is a teacher in my life." Instead of saying you have pain, you call the pain a "signal." Because the truth is, when you have pain, it's trying to tell you something.

Pain Can Be Your Friend

If you pay attention to the pain, you can learn something. Most people who are victims when they have pain just want to put out the fire; they want to put out the pain. But if you find out what origi-nated that pain, you can actually remove it forever. So pain can become a signal. Instead of saying, "I demand," you can say, "I would

appreciate." It's kinder and much more loving. Instead of saying you
have a complaint, you can say, "I have a request." Instead of saying
you are struggling, you can say, "I'm on a journey." Instead of saying,
"You did this!" again sounding like a victim, you can say, "I created
this." These are all ways to work within this first stage of awakening.
You're working with language, you're working with thought, you're
working with your mind, but this is where it all begins. We have
all been victims, myself included—there's nothing negative about it,
and you're not to blame. You're waking up; you're taking responsibility; you're going forward. You should actually pat yourself on the
back because you're doing so great; you should reward yourself for
what you are doing and how you are investing in your own life.

Go for Your Dreams

This is all about encouraging you to go for your dreams. I am a guy
who looks for ways to encourage myself and others. But it wasn't
always that way. When I was growing up, as I said earlier, I was mad
at everybody. Yet as I encountered people who believed in me, people
who encouraged me, who pulled something out of me, something
great, something that was deep within me that just needed to be dusted
off and shined a little bit, and watered, and put in a little sunlight
until it started to grow, it started to make a difference. I'm doing that
with you. I'm encouraging you. Somebody asked me recently where
I started to learn about encouragement and why it is so important,
and how did I learn that it made such a difference in your life when
you start to encourage yourself and encourage the people around you.
Then I thought about it, and I remembered that I read a book,
probably in the 1980s, called *The Marva Collins Way*.

Marva Collins was a Chicago schoolteacher, and she was working in the inner city in a ghetto area. She was working for the school
system, and she was absolutely frustrated with the system to the point

that she quit. She opened up her own school in the upper floor of her own house. She had five kids to begin with. Two of them were her own children. The kids she took were the ones who were basically thrown away by the system. These kids were thought of as retarded, "special." They were illiterate; they were not teachable in any way, shape, or form—according to the school system, anyway. Marva took them in, and she encouraged them. And the book taught me that what she really did was love them. She loved those kids when they did not really love themselves, when they were, in many ways, victims of their own households. And some of the parents believed in Marva enough to drop off their kids there.

Marva taught those kids how to read, how to write. She taught them Shakespeare. She taught them to read poetry, to write poetry, to speak poetry. She had them tested after a year of being with her, and all of those kids tested five grades higher than all the other children around them. *The Marva Collins Way* actually became so popular that she opened a big school. She was able to take 200 kids, but there was a waiting list of 800 children. Now, this is pretty mind-boggling. But the essence of what she was doing was taking people who were considered to be victims and loving them, encouraging them, finding the good in them. She didn't criticize them if they did something wrong; she rewarded them if they did something right.

The other person I studied was Win Wenger, who wrote a book called *The Einstein Factor*. I absolutely love Win. I think he's an Einstein in his own right. He's a genius. He encourages people and teaches people how to increase their IQ. Most people think their IQ is pretty much set in stone; again, that's a victim mentality. But Win teaches people imaginary techniques, or imagery techniques, and by practicing about 20 minutes a day, they can increase their IQ by numerous points. It's very surprising. Win said, and he taught me the first law of psychology, which is that you get more of whatever you focus on. When he saw people who were doing something good, he applauded that. When Marva Collins saw that somebody was doing something good, she applauded that. That encouragement enlarged what those people focused on. Whatever you focus on is going to expand.

Focus on What's Right in Your World

Now, this is very relevant, because if you focus on what's wrong in your world, if you focus on being a victim, if you focus on being negative, you are going to expand on all of that. There's nothing hokey about that; it's actually the first law of psychology, according to Win. And this whole method of encouraging yourself, finding something good, loving yourself, finding something to love in yourself, is a way to begin to blossom and emerge out of this first stage of awakening. You begin to leave victimhood behind, because then you will find that you have more power, more creativity, more control, and more to love than you ever imagined before.

I started using "The Marva Collins Way" and "The Win Wenger Way" in my own life when I started teaching classes in Houston—adult education classes on writing and publishing. I'd use the same method. I found that when people who thought they were victims (destined to be a certain way in their life because of the programming of their DNA) were actually encouraged, they did miraculous things. They got published when they thought they couldn't get published. One woman who came to my classes had not written a thing since she'd been in high school, because when she wrote something for her father, he thought it was absolutely horrible and tore it up, and she was traumatized from the event. She was feeling like a victim.

Thirty years later, she took my class, and I showed her some ways to write, and I encouraged her to be a writer. I encouraged her to breathe through the experience that she had of being a victim, and she ended up writing a book. And the book was actually outstanding. I don't know if it was ever published, but she did move forward by finding somebody who believed in her. I created a Miracles Coaching program based on all these principles so that people can have access to somebody who will encourage them, who will believe in them.

Believe in Yourself

My point for you is this: You have to believe in yourself. If you take a good, hard look at yourself, you can find the good, the bad, and the ugly. I want you to focus on the good. I want you to begin to blossom within this first stage of awakening by finding out what your positive traits are.

Inventory Your Strengths

In fact, a wise thing to do when you get a chance is make a list of all your strengths. These are the things you know you're good at or that other people say you're good at. These are the things that you love to do no matter what; these are the things you would do whether you were paid or not. This could be anything from singing to playing to gardening to working out to learning or speaking a language. It could be any number of things. It could be working on cars. It could be anything. I want you to focus on whatever you feel is a positive trait, and I want you to take an inventory of it. This is the way to acknowledge your good, to acknowledge your skills, to focus on the positive in you, because when you focus on it, remember, it's going to expand, and it's a way to begin to love yourself.

There's Always a Positive Reason

What I'd like you to do now is to make a list of all the moments and times in your past when you felt like a victim. Remember, you're just taking an inventory. This doesn't have to be a traumatic experience.

Just have a little bit of fun with it; just breathe. Breathing is very important. Taking two or three breaths as you do any exercise is going to make it easier for you. Involve the body; stretch a little bit. Go ahead and move the shoulders a little bit; push up; sit up straight in your chair; take a deep breath, and let it out slowly. Just let yourself relax into this exercise.

You're making this list of experiences or moments in which you felt like a victim. After you've made that list, go ahead and pick one item, and let me walk you through what we do with it. Just scan the list and pick out anything that stands out. It doesn't matter at which you choose; there's no right or wrong. One of them is there; you pick it; you choose it; you welcome it.

What I'd like you to do is have a dialogue with it. You can have a dialogue on paper if you like, or you can have a dialogue in your mind. What you're going to do is to ask the experience itself what it has to teach you. You're going to assume there's a positive reason for what occurred. Again, remember to breathe. You're safe; you're relaxing; all is well in the world. You've controlled your situation and your circumstances; you're at peace. It's safe to look at this.

Okay, you've picked an item off your list, something that happened in the past, and now you're looking at it with a little bit of detachment. And you're pretending that the experience can actually talk to you. I know it sounds odd, but if you just pretend, if you just imagine, if it does tell you the meaning for it, what might it say? Whatever you feel or hear or intuit, just welcome it. Don't judge it; don't criticize it; don't question it. Let it be.

Again, ask that particular experience the reason for it. What might have been the good cause behind it? Whatever comes to mind is okay. If you have difficulty hearing the answer, just pretend that there's an answer. If you pretend that the experience can talk, and you pretend that there is actually a positive reason for the event, what might that be? Note whatever comes up. If for some reason, nothing feels like it's coming up, just relax with that, because very often it will come to you later. You might be walking around; you might be watching TV; you might even get an answer in your dreams. Trust that it will come. You've stated this intention, that you welcome the good reason, the positive reason, for the event listed on your inventory.

So it will come. If it doesn't come right now, that's okay. If it does come now, or whenever it does come, write it down. Acknowledge it. Go ahead and put it in your notebook. Then, when you feel like it, you can go through the same process for each and every one of the other items on your list. You don't have to do them all at once; you don't have to do them all right now. You can take your time and do these at your leisure. Have fun with them. Actually know that you're safe, and just relax. All of the events are over with. What you're looking for is the positive reason for their occurrence.

If you didn't receive the message right now, just enjoy the relaxing, positive state of total love. I'll see you in the next chapter of *The Awakening Course.*

Chapter 3

Stage Two
Empowerment

The universe likes speed. When the intuitive nudge from within is there, act. You know in your heart that you want to do something. It might be to open a business; it might be to open a service; it might be to write a book; it might be to do any number of things, but unique to you.

—Joe Vitale

Welcome to Stage Two, Empowerment. I'm very excited to be here, because you are growing through the stages of enlightenment. You are becoming more and more aware. You are becoming more and more awake.

From Victim to Wizard

In this next stage, something really magical happens, because you begin to become a wizard of your own life. Now, how do you go from being a victim to being empowered? How do you go from that first stage to the second stage?

What happens is, along the way you see a movie, you read a book, somebody says the right thing, you attend the right seminar, you listen to the right audio program, and something pops. Something awakens. And I have to tell you that a movie called *The Secret* has done that for a lot of people. It came out, I believe, in 2006, and it swept the United States and then swept across the planet. It has been single-handedly awakening everybody who watches it, or virtually everybody, anyway.

What is *The Secret*? First of all, if you don't know about it, you can go to www.thesecret.tv and read all about it. Even watch some of it, download it if you want, or buy the DVD. It is worth watching.

The Law of Attraction

The Secret is about the Law of Attraction. Let me introduce that to you. The Law of Attraction is the principal that everything you're getting in your life, you are attracting because of your unconscious beliefs. Your energy, your beliefs, your mind-set, your unconscious system is pulling it into your life experience.

If this is the first time you've heard it, it's probably going to be a bit of a shock, because you start to think, "Oh my God, I'm responsible for this mess? I'm responsible for everything I've got in my life, good, bad, and indifferent?" Yes, you are. But the good news is that you weren't doing it consciously. You were doing it unconsciously, so there's no reason to beat yourself up. You didn't know what you were doing. In many ways, you were still acting as a victim.

Then along comes the movie *The Secret,* which says that you can virtually have whatever you want, if you can imagine it with feeling. That's the good news in all of this, that you can virtually turn your life around by focusing on what you want, with feeling, and acting in what I call an inspired way, to bring it to you.

Let me clarify how all this works. I was able to get a role in *The Secret* because I wrote a book called *The Attractor Factor. The Attractor Factor* reveals five steps for creating wealth or anything else you want in your life.

It's very useful to go through those five steps right now, because it gives you a basis from which to learn the rest of *The Secret.* And we're also going to build on it, then leave it behind. But for now, in this second stage, you need to know it.

**The Attractor Factor Process: Five Steps for Creating
Anything You Want**

What are the five steps? The first step is to know what you *don't*
want. That's where most people are. They're pretty clear about what
they don't want. They complain about their jobs. If they're entrepreneurs, they complain about their lack of business. Or they complain
about their health, or their relationships, or their finances. They just
plain complain.

1. *Know What You Don't Want*

I say that it is fine and useful to know what you don't want. It is
the first step in *The Attractor Factor* process. Knowing what you don't
want is useful information. So take note of it. In fact, you might even
want to write it down. Take all of what you say you don't want and
turn it into what you do want.

2. *Declare an Intention: What Do You Want?*

The second step is to declare an intention. You're declaring what you
want. Some people say, "I don't know what I want." All they have
to do is look at what they're complaining about and turn it into an
affirmation. Turn it into a goal. Turn it into an intention.

If you catch yourself saying something like, "Oh, I just hate my
job," you want to turn it into something that says, "I intend to love
my job," or "I intend to attract the job I do love." If you say something like, "I'm really tired of not having enough money to pay my
house bill, or my phone bill, or my car bill," whatever it happens to
be, that's your complaint. What do you want?

You turn it into what your statement of intent is. It could be, "I
want to have more than enough money to pay my bills on time or
before they're due," or you could say, "I even intend to pay all of my
bills off completely and be debt free."

As you can see, you use the first step to get to the second step.

So, the first step is listing what you don't want. The second step is transforming that "don't want," into what you do want, your intention. Oprah Winfrey says, "Intention rules the earth." I'll talk more about that as we go through this particular chapter.

3. Clear Limiting Beliefs

What is the third step? The third step is very profound. It's very important. It's something almost nobody talks about. It's called "get clear." What does that mean? It means that if you have counterintentions, or negative beliefs, or issues with deservedness and self-confidence within you, you will actually block the receiving of the very thing you want.

In the second step, you may have said, "I intend to lose weight." "I intend to stop smoking." "I intend to attract great wealth." However, if inside of you, you don't believe that's possible, or you don't believe you deserve it, or you have any number of beliefs that are limiting, negative beliefs, you will block the intention from coming about.

So, in the third step, you have to get clear of the negativity. You have to get clear of the limiting beliefs. You have to get clear of the stuff that is stopping you, stuff that's in your unconscious mind.

This is what most people don't have a clue about, and most people never talk about, because they're not aware of it. This is good news. When you get clear, you can virtually have anything you want, and you can have it almost instantaneously. That's the promise of step three.

4. "Nevillize" Your Goal

The fourth step in *The Attractor Factor* process is something called "Nevillize Your Goal." I coined the word *Nevillize*. It's based on a man named Neville Goddard, who was a mystic, an author, a speaker. He talked about attracting into your life whatever you wanted, when you could visualize the end result of it with feeling. The key to Nevillizing your goal is this feeling aspect. A lot of people know about visualization, they know about meditation (if you don't, I'll talk to you a little bit about it in this chapter), but Nevillizing your goal goes beyond all of that. In this fourth step, you imagine the end result.

If you want more money in your life, if you want that car, if you want that particular house or particular job or a certain person to be in better heath, you visualize having it now. This doesn't mean you visualize having it in the future; you pretend that you already have it in this moment. When you pretend it's already come to pass, you actually accelerate the Law of Attraction, and it begins to come into your life. By Nevillizing your goal, you make it more real to you, and you make it more real to the universe. The universe will then supply it to you. That's the fourth step: "Nevillize Your Goal."

5. Let Go and Take Inspired Action

What is step five? Let go while taking inspired action. That means that you're letting go of your attachment. Remember those seven principles I talked about earlier? When you can let go of your need, your addiction, your attachment to wanting something, and just allow it to come into your being, it comes to you much more quickly. You don't have any roadblocks in the way of it.

Letting go means that you let go of your need for something to happen. You want the job, you want the wealth, you want the health, you want the car—whatever it happens to be that you desire. But you won't die if you don't get it, so you have this relaxed expectation about you. It's a certain state of playfulness. The other part of letting go to "take inspired action." This is very important. A lot of people have seen the movie *The Secret,* and they criticize it by saying, "*The Secret* doesn't talk about taking action. *The Secret* just says, 'Oh, if I sit in a chair, and I visualize having a car, when I get out of the chair, the car will be in my parking lot.'" It doesn't work like that.

I definitely believe in magic and miracles, and something like that is possible. But more often than not, you have to do something. You actually have to take action. You have to participate in the manifestation process, because it's a cocreation process. You do something, and the universe, or the Divine, or God—whatever you want to call the power higher than yourself—also kicks in and does its part. It's a joint effort here.

So, you have to take what I call *inspired action*. That's the fifth step. And inspired action is something that comes from within you. It's not somebody saying, "Oh, you have to write a business plan," or "You have to take out an ad to find a particular person or to get a particular job." Instead, focus on this: What does your intuition from within tell you to do? It might nudge you to buy a book, to attend a seminar, to turn left one day when you normally turn right. It will nudge you from within. It's inspired, because it's coming from inside of you.

The Power Is in You

These are the five steps in *The Attractor Factor* process. You can use them on virtually anything. It's all part of being empowered. It's all part of realizing that you have more power than you ever imagined. As a victim, you never felt that way. You were working within the mind-set of "you against the world," and that's how it felt. It was frustrating, and it was irritating, and it was draining on you.

You see the movie *The Secret*. You learn about the Law of Attraction. You read *The Attractor Factor*—and any number of books that have come out since *The Secret*. There are all kinds of books and all kinds of great authors. You start to realize, "Wow, I've got power surging through me! With my mind, with my visualization, I can actually achieve by-God miracles!" That's the fun, the glory, and the magic of this particular stage.

Putting It into Practice

Let's have a little fun. I'd like you to imagine something you'd like to have in your life right now. Something you'd like to attract. This will make the sense of empowerment really real for you right now.

So, *imagine.* Is it a car? Is it a relationship? Is it health? Is it a house? Is it something else that I'm not naming here, yet something you've always longed to have? It doesn't have to be gigantic. It doesn't have to be something that you think is impossible. Let it be a little bit of a stretch for you, but something that you would really welcome into your life. What would you like to attract right now?

One way to hone in on that is to think of the first step in *The Attractor Factor.* What have you been complaining about? If you said, "I'm tired of having a backache," then obviously you want to focus on perfect health. You want to focus on having a strong back. Think about what you've been complaining about, and then pick that. Whatever *that* happens to be. There's no right or wrong. Whatever your desire happens to be is fine. Then you're going to turn it into an intention, a statement, something that you intend to have.

Wanting something is just fine, but I feel it's stronger if you say, "I intend to have this money." "I intend to have unexpected income." "I intend to fix my health." *I intend* is stronger and more empowering than just saying, "*I want* to have more money."

As you think about what you desire, and as you start to imagine having it, note whether any thoughts come up in regard to it. For example, if you think, "I want to have this particular car," but the thought comes up, "How will I ever afford that?" or "What will my parents think if I get this particular car?" or "What will my neighbors think if I get this particular car?" "Will I go on the radar of thieves if I get this particular car?" Any number of beliefs are going to come up. Let them be, for now, just note them. When you get to your desk, you might write them down. But for now, just welcome them. Remember to breathe. Notice what the beliefs are.

Let's continue, then, and go to the fourth step. This is where you imagine that you already have the thing you intend to attract to you. At this point, you are visualizing the end result. You are imagining that it's already done. If it is the car, it's in your driveway. If it is health, you've gone to the doctor and the doctor has said, "You are totally fine!" You are cleared of whatever the obstruction happened to have been. In whatever way possible, find the end result of the attraction for this particular experience.

If you've been wanting this new house, and you said, "I intend to have this house," you took care of the beliefs that were coming up that talked about deservedness and how you will pay for it. You simply acknowledged them and let them go. Now you're at the stage where you're visualizing that you own the house. You can see yourself walking into the house, and that feels fantastic.

Get into the feelings of the end result. This is very important in Nevillizing your goal. The end result is what matters. It's not how you're attracting it to you; you're just imagining that it's already been attracted to you. Enjoy that for a moment. Then, just breathe and let it go.

You breathe and let it go, because the fifth step is let go while taking inspired action. You'll notice, over the next few minutes, few hours, or few days, that you'll get ideas to do something. You'll get suggestions to do something. They'll come from within you. You'll get these little nudges. Act on those nudges, because those nudges are coming from the bigger part of you that sees the universe.

Your conscious mind, your ego, can only see through a tiny hole in a porthole. The actual experience of living in the universe is more appropriate to your unconscious mind. The intuitive will come from your unconscious. It may actually come from the *collective unconscious,* to use a Carl Jung term, and bubble up through your unconscious into your conscious mind.

Whether or not that makes sense to you, just understand that you're going to be getting impulses, intuitive nudges to do something.

I am challenging you to do them, because when you do them, they'll take you in the direction of creating or attracting the thing you want to manifest.

That's how simple this is. That's how simply this works. And that's how profound this is.

Expand Your Thinking

Now I want to challenge you. I said earlier that I want you to dare something worthy. Well, I want you to think of something big right now. I did ask you, a little earlier, to pick something small to process through these five steps. Now I want to expand your thinking. I want you to start entertaining the idea that miracles are, indeed, possible and to let me prove it to you.

Beyond Incurable

Meir Schneider is a fellow who was born blind. He has a certificate of blindness that he can show you. Not only that, he can read it to you. *He can read it to you.* He now drives a car in California. He now has a school where he has taught hundreds, if not thousands, of people to see again.

He's improved vision of people with impaired vision, and he's improved the vision of people who were blind. In Meir's own case, when doctors look at his eyes and study his lenses, they say that it is impossible for him to see, that he doesn't have the structure in his eyes to be able to focus on anything.

He sees. I interviewed him. I put him on the cover of *East/West Journal* magazine back in 1984 or 1985. He's still around today. He's still teaching people. He's still driving. He's still reading. He's still inspiring people.

Well, people say blindness is incurable. What's the story with Meir? What about autism? People say autism is not curable. You can find exceptions to that. But for the longest time, people have thought that if you have an autistic child, then that's it—you are not going to be able to do anything about it.

Take Barry and Suzi Kaufman, for example. A long time ago, one of their kids was born autistic. They didn't accept what the medical community said. Because the medical community said, "You can't work with this child." "You have other children; focus on them." "I'm sorry that you have an autistic child." The Kaufmans didn't accept that. They believe in miracles. They believe in love. They practiced total self-acceptance. They practiced love with their little son Ron. They did it for seven years. Ron is no longer autistic. He is a fully grown adult. Ron also graduated from a major university. He has no signs of autism, and he runs a corporation today. Well, I thought autism was incurable?

"Impossible" Is Just a Word

I'm pointing out to you that people who come from a victim mentality believe that whatever others have said is impossible is truly impossible. When you leave that behind and start to feel that you're empowered, you realize that "impossible" just might be a vague term and that if you test the limits of it, you just might be able to do things that are, in the eyes of everybody else, impossible.

Cure blindness; cure autism; cure anything. Fill in the blank. I'm challenging you. I'm challenging you to think of something big. You might be a little resistant because you have to use step three, which is to "get clear." The resistance means that your beliefs say, "Hmm, I don't know if that's possible. I don't know whether I can pull that off. I don't know whether I have the funds to do that. I don't know if that's possible in the world of physics."

All of those are beliefs, and they can be cleared.

How to "Get Clear"

How do you clear beliefs? This is an important part in the movie *The Secret,* in the whole Law of Attraction movement, and in my own book, *The Attractor Factor.* It's the idea that you must get clear. When you get clear, you can get results. But how do you get clear?

Focus on Gratitude

There are a couple of things I like to do. One of them is to focus on gratitude. That might seem a little strange, and I know when I first heard it 20-odd years ago I thought, "Yeah, I'll be grateful when I have something to be grateful for." But that's not how it works. In fact, you have to look at what you have *right now* and realize that, no matter where you are and what you have, you're actually pretty wealthy.

I gave a talk once called "The AAA Plan to Wealth." The first *A* stood for Already. You are *already* wealthy. I had people stop, look at their lives, and realize that they had some sort of transportation, some sort of food, some sort of security, some sort of roof over their head. They probably had an income. Maybe it was unemployment compensation, but they had something. If they compared it to people in Third World countries, if they compared it to people who were actually kings and queens of countries in past times, they were actually doing very well.

So, you are wealthy right now. You are actually doing far better than you imagine. What you're striving for is *more.* And this program will help you achieve more, but one of the ways in which you can start attracting more into your life is to be grateful for what you have now.

When I first heard this, I was very skeptical. Maybe like you. I remember picking up a pencil and thinking, "Well, I'll try this gratitude thing." I picked up a pencil, and I thought (a little bit flippantly), "Well, I guess with this pencil, which, on the one hand, has lead in it, I can write anything from a grocery list to a suicide note to the great American novel to a play to a love letter—to any number of things." And I thought, "Well, that's actually a pretty cool invention, you know? I can be creative with this piece of lead." Then I looked at the other end of the pencil, and I thought, "Well, what an ingenious little piece of rubber that is," because whatever I wrote and I didn't like, I just erased away.

As I looked at that pencil, and maybe you could hear it in my voice, I started to feel truly grateful for it. I started to think that the pencil was actually like a magic wand. I could write out intentions; I could write out complaints; I could write out love letters; I could write out suicide notes. I mean, I could do any number of things with this object, and then I could erase them if I wished.

Well, feeling grateful for that pencil opened my heart just a little bit to allow the love of the universe to come in. It goes back to the principal I spoke of earlier: You get more of whatever you focus on.

When I began to focus on gratitude, I began to draw into my life more things and experiences to be grateful for. This became pretty magical and pretty cool, because all I did was just stop, look around, and say, "What am I grateful for right now?" It could have been for the person I was talking to; it could have been for what I just ate; it could have been for the fact that I can breathe, and I'm alive, and everything's working in my body. As I felt grateful for that, I washed away any negativity within me. It brought me into the moment, and it brought me into this spirit of happiness, and it brought me into the realization that *now* is actually pretty cool. And when I realized that now is actually pretty complete and cool, all by itself, I became able to attract more of the same, or even better.

One of my favorite clearing techniques is simply to feel gratitude.

The Story of Kirk

Let me tell you a little story about Kirk. Kirk is probably, at this point, a nine-year-old little boy. Kirk had a pediatric stroke six weeks after birth. Many elderly people have strokes. I didn't know that children could have them, too. But Kirk had one, which was devastating to his family. I heard about it through a mutual friend, and I wanted to help.

I donated a lot of money to Kirk's family, and his mother sends me photos of Kirk. Every time I get one, Kirk is smiling. When I see that smile, I start to beam, and I think, "Oh, life is truly wonderful." Kirk's mom writes and tells me that Kirk is not unhappy about his situation at all. The people who are unhappy are the people who look at him and imagine what it's like. But Kirk, in his own body, in his own mind, is actually a little Buddha. He is actually at peace. He's grateful. He's grateful to be alive.

So I look at little Kirk and I start feeling gratitude. I start feeling as though this is what it's all about. To accept who you are, where you are, while still trying to make a difference. You are trying to walk, if you can't walk. If you've had a stroke, you're trying to repair your system, just like little Kirk is doing. And he's doing it joyfully. He's doing it with a spirit of gratitude, one of, "I'm glad to be alive." It reminds me to be grateful for what I have. And I'm reminding you to be grateful for what you have.

A Clue to Your Millions

It's one of the most powerful attractors, and it's one of the most powerful clearing techniques you can imagine. If you're feeling that you can't be grateful right now, and you have a lot of thoughts that are negative, or if you have a lot of complaints in your mind, well, guess what? That's actually good.

You know, I was on Donny Deutsch's CNBC TV show, *The Big Idea*. It was one of the proud moments of my life, and I'm glad I attracted that experience, and I think he's doing great work. But if you watch his show, he repeatedly tells you that your wealth, your gold, your financial freedom—in his particular case—is in whatever you're complaining about.

He says to look around when you say something like, "Wow, I wish they would fix this," or "I wish somebody would do something about this," or "I wish somebody would provide this." He says, "Ding-ding. That's a clue to your millions."

Well, it's the same thing if you're sitting there right now thinking, "I can't feel grateful. You know, I've got all these problems going on." It's actually okay. You can accept them, you can actually welcome them, and you can truly even be grateful for them.

You can turn them around, as we go through this process, but it's okay to think and feel whatever you are thinking and feeling right now.

Become a Belief Detective

Let me talk about one of the other clearing techniques that's actually one of my all-time favorites, and I use it all the time. It's a belief clearing technique, where you become a belief detective.

It's very important to know what your beliefs are, because your beliefs are creating your reality. When you're trying to attract something into your life, and you feel like you're not pulling it in, it's because you have an unconscious counterintention. And you want to find out what that counterintention is.

To make this crystal clear for you, let me offer the following: Most people on January 1 set intentions for their lives. They may say something like, "I want to lose weight," "I want to stop smoking," "I want to start working out three times a week," or whatever it happens to be. But what happens the next day, or the next week? They forget all about their intentions.

This is very important, because you may think, "Well, if intentions rule the earth, how come when I set an intention on January 1, and I really want it, it doesn't happen?"

Most people set very positive, healthy intentions. They don't say, for example, "I'm going to start shooting heroin tomorrow." Instead, they say something like, "I'm going to go look for a job," "I'm going to start my business," or whatever it happens to be that's positive and well intentioned. They don't do it because of counterintentions. They have a counterbelief in their unconscious mind that's more powerful. It's vetoing and overriding the stated conscious resolution.

Again, how do you clear that? You do it by becoming a belief detective, and here's how it works. You have the belief that pops up. And it's going to pop up because it shows up in your mind; it shows up in your conversation; it shows up in statements like, "This always happens to me," "I'll never have enough money," "This is just how I'm destined to be," "Men are always like this," "Women are always like that." There's a belief there, and when you hear the belief, you want to question it. You want to say, "Do I believe it?"

If you have the belief that says, "I never have enough money," okay, that's a belief. Pause, and ask yourself, "Do I believe that I never have enough money?" And you might find yourself saying, "No, I don't believe that." If so, let it go. It's probably not an active belief. But if you say, "Yes, I do believe that I don't have enough money. I never have enough money," that's fine. Your next question is, "Why do I believe that?"

What you're fishing for is your own evidence, for your own belief. As you go through this questioning process, and you go a little bit deeper, you'll find the bottom-line evidence. It might have come from your parents. It might have been your mother and father at a moment when their paycheck was less then they expected, or they couldn't pay their grocery bills. And in that moment, they may have said something like, "There's never enough money." You heard it and took it in, unquestioningly, because at that point you didn't have the awareness to question it. Now you do.

Question Everything

As you question your beliefs to get to the bottom-line evidence, you'll find a great sense of freedom. You'll feel empowered. You'll feel empowered because you have a choice. At that juncture, you can say, "I want to continue believing that," or you can say, "That belief isn't serving me, and I'm going to go ahead and replace it, or just let it go."

That's the power of this questioning process. I advise you to do this lovingly, gently. Not angrily. Not with frustration. Just have fun with it. Pretend you're Sherlock Holmes and you're going on a "belief hunt." Just ask yourself, "What do I believe about money?" "What do I believe about relationships?" "What do I believe about health?" and accept whatever comes up. There's no right or wrong. They're just beliefs.

Whatever comes up, note it, maybe write it down. Then question it. "Do I believe that?" If you do, it's okay. If you do, you can say, "Why do I believe that?" Let whatever comes up be okay, as well. When it comes up, you can ask yourself, "Do I believe this evidence?" If you say no, it's probably finished. If you say yes, you can ask, "Why do I believe this evidence? Why do I want to continue believing this belief?"

Something else will come up. You can question that. In other words, just dig here and have fun with it. It's very powerful to do this in writing. You can always do it out loud. I started a whole Miracles Coaching program; I trained coaches to do this with people who want to break through in their own lives.

You can do this yourself. You can do it on this session; you can do it with paper and pen; you can do it out loud sitting under a tree somewhere. As you do it, you free yourself to change reality.

"Is It Really True?"

Let me tell you a quick story about this. I struggled, for the longest time, with finances. As I've already mentioned (probably too many times), I was homeless at one point, and it struggled in poverty for a long time. I had issues with money. And as it became clear that money is actually okay, that I can actually make a difference in my life, in my family's life, in the world (if I so chose) with the money I bring in, I started to pull in more money.

Most people have the belief that the more money they spend, the less money they have. I believed that myself, until I questioned it. *I questioned it.* How many people stop and question a belief like, "The more money I spend, the less money I have"? It feels obvious; it feels like reality. Most accountants would agree with this statement. But I questioned it, and I thought, "I wonder if that's actually true?"

If I'm living in an empowered state of awareness, and I realize that I am cocreating my reality, and if we actually live in a belief-created universe, what if I question that belief? What if I question any belief?

Well, I questioned that one, and I realized it's not necessarily true. I changed it to: "The more money I spend, the more money I receive." That is now my reality. I cannot dispose of money fast enough. "The more money I spend, the more money I receive" is my way of being.

I can't explain that in any logical way, any more than what I'm doing right now, because it's happening in this unconscious connection to a magical universe. As I spend money on whatever I want, there's no end to the money. I've given money, as I've mentioned, to Kirk's mother. I've given money to causes I believe in; I've started my own causes; and I've bought toys and cars for myself. I've done all kinds of wonderful things for wonderful people, including me. And as I've done that, the money keeps coming. Why? What's the difference in my life now versus earlier? The difference is that I have changed the active belief. On the one hand, "The more money I spend, the less money I have" seemed like a natural belief, until I questioned it. Now I have one that says, "The more money I spend, the more money I receive." I like that belief a lot better.

What Are You Grateful For?

Well, we were just talking about receiving, so it's time for you to make a gratitude list.

This is something you can do on paper, or you can actually do it mentally. I'd like for you to begin small: Look around and just ask yourself, "What am I grateful for?"

It could be the fact that you're breathing. And, as you're thinking about that, just take a deep breath. Hold it for a second and release it. Appreciate how good that feels. You can be grateful for the fact that you are breathing. You are alive in this wonderful time, reading this wonderful material, relaxing to my words as you take an inventory of your life.

Mentally or, if you're at your desk, physically make a list of everything that you are grateful for.

It could be for your hands, for your legs, your face, your hair. It could be for all the people in your life, for the work that you have in your life. It could be for your vehicle. It could be for your home; it could be for your neighbors. It could be for your city, your state, your country. It could be for something as small as a pencil.

Just make a short (or long) list of all the things you're grateful for. Again, you're doing this mentally.

It's the Feeling That Matters

Get into the feel of it. The feeling is what really matters.

As you make this list, notice what you're grateful for. Almost every night, I get into a hot tub. As I'm in that hot tub, I'm reflecting on my life, and I'm making a mental list of everything I'm grateful for. And as I truly start to move into the spirit of deep gratitude, I almost start to cry, because I'm so profoundly grateful for what's going on in my life. I am inviting you to do the same thing.

Look around and say, "I might want things to be different. I want more of certain things in my life, but the truth is, right now, all is well. And right now, I have abundance. Right now, I have a long list of things to be grateful for." Mentally, welcome that list into your mind, and physically, write it down the first chance you get. This is very powerful.

You Attract More of What You Are Grateful For

As I said earlier, you get more of whatever you focus on. As you focus on gratitude, you will attract more to be grateful for. This is a primary rule in psychology. It's a fact, and it's a reality. And it will be your reality as you focus on what you're grateful for.

You can look at your body, and within your body, there are probably some parts that you really, truly, love. Maybe it's your thighs, your arms, your legs, your face. There's *something* there, maybe your eyes. Maybe it's the color of your hair. Whatever it is, focus on what you love about your body. Just take a mental inventory, and later you can write this down.

Then look at your home. Wherever you are, you have things that you're grateful for. It could be a comfy chair or sofa. It could be your TV set. It could be your DVD player. It could be the windows. It could be the way the house faces the street. There's something there that you truly, truly love—and probably some area that you're really grateful for within the house. Maybe you're there now.

Look at your family. You have friends. You have neighbors. You have family. Look at your parents. Look at the aspects of all of these people and all of these categories, and focus on what you love about them. Focus on what you're grateful for. Again, get into the feeling. *Feel* this gratitude.

Think about past experiences. Maybe you can call up something that was truly wonderful in your life, something that you love remembering. Maybe it was something that made you laugh. Something where you felt deep love or deep gratitude. An experience you shared with friends, an experience you love to remember. As you focus on that, notice the feelings of gratitude: Just let them well up within you; breathe into them; enjoy them.

Notice your work. There are probably aspects of your work that you absolutely love. Maybe it is the type of work you do. Maybe it's where you are working. Maybe it's your salary. Maybe it's the benefits. There's something in your work that you truly are grateful for. Look around. Maybe there are business opportunities that you're grateful for. Maybe there's one that you haven't acted on, but you're excited about. Maybe there's one that you have acted on, and you're doing well with, and you're very grateful for.

Look in the area of travel and recreation. Maybe you took a vacation. Maybe you want to take a vacation. Notice how you feel when you start to feel gratitude for the travel you've done, the vacations you've taken, the recreation you've enjoyed. Maybe there are hobbies. Maybe you have certain pastimes that you are really good at or really enjoy doing. Or maybe are very relaxed when you do them.

Whatever the case, just take your inventory. This is a list of gratitude moments. This is a list you can refer to over and over again. It's like a touchstone for your life. As you think about the things you are grateful for, it will pull up more experiences. It will magnetize other experiences that come into your awareness. As they do, note them, thank them for showing up, and write them down in your journal when you have a chance.

Again, be grateful for it all. Be grateful for this moment. Be grateful for the gratitude exercise itself.

We're all perfect. I'm glad you're in this feeling of gratitude, because this is a great place. It's a launching pad to do something big. Now I'm going to ask you to close your eyes. When you're comfortable, safe, and secure, proceed with the following exercise, and be sure to write down what happens. Go ahead, tune in . . . and relax.

Meditation: Make Your Life Bigger

Earlier in this chapter, I dared you to do something worthy. Then I talked about Meir Schneider overcoming blindness. And about Barry Kaufman and his wife overcoming autism in their child. I want you to dare something worthy. I want you to think of something big.

You are now in the stage of being empowered, and in this stage, I want you to think bigger than you've ever thought before. I want you to dare something worthy.

I want you to go through your life and imagine what would you do if you could not fail? What would you do if you were fearless? What would you do if you could do anything? What would you go for?

For the purposes of this meditation, just pick anything. Something big, something bold. Something exciting, something daring. Now I want you to imagine what it would be like to achieve it. You don't have to worry about *how* to achieve it—just let that go for right now. You don't need to know that. Go to the end result. You have done it. You have manifested it. You have attracted it. Somehow, some way, it's now in your experience.

What does that feel like? What does it feel like in your body? Do you feel that tingle of excitement? Is your breathing a little bit more rapid because you are excited about this? Are you smiling? Are you sharing this with somebody? How does this feel all through your body? What do you sense? If you could reach out and touch something, what would it feel like? Have you touched the end result? What is it like to live it? To wear it? To feel it? To be it?

For a moment, just relish in all this wonderful bodily sense of feeling. You have achieved something that others might have said was impossible. You have done something big. You have dared something worthy.

Get into the end result. You are there. You've already accomplished it. It feels wonderful. You can't wait to share this with others. You can't wait to talk about this. You can't wait to write about this. You're probably going to draft a whole essay about what it feels like to experience the manifestation of this big goal or intention of yours.

Just for a moment, simply listen and enjoy, and relish this wonderful experience of having manifested something truly great in your life.

Congratulations. You did it.

Chapter 4

Stage Three
Surrender

"I'm sorry. Please forgive me. Thank you. I love you."

It doesn't matter what order you say the phrases in. The idea is to say them. Follow your inspiration and say them within yourself in the order that feels best. Let your feelings be your guide. In the last Zero Limits event, Dr. Hew Len shortened the four phrases to just two: "I love you" and "Thank you."

—Joe Vitale

W elcome to Stage Three in *The Awakening Course,* which is about surrender.

But That's Impossible: The H'oponopono Story

What usually happens along the way, what usually helps you awaken to each one of these stages, is something like a story. I had this happen to me several years ago. A friend of mine told me a story, and I didn't believe it at first. He told me this story about a therapist who worked for a mental hospital for the criminally insane. He said this therapist, somehow, some way, used a Hawaiian healing technique and helped heal every one of those inmates, those patients. The punch line was, he didn't even see any of them.

I thought, "This isn't possible." I know about magic and miracles. I know about remote healing. I know about distance healing, and Reiki this, and energy that. I just didn't feel that this was possible. So I dismissed it, which shows you how open-minded I've been in the past. Then, a year after that, I heard the same story. My friend who had told me this story said, "Did you ever check it out? Did you ever go find the therapist who healed all those mentally ill criminals?"

I said, "No. I more or less dismissed it."

He said, "Let's go online right now." We had a laptop computer, and we turned it on and started looking around. We found it very difficult to find information, at least at that point in time. We kept looking, and we did find a name.

I didn't do anything at that point, but a few days later, when I was back on my own computer, in the comfort of my own home, I started really wondering about this therapist and this method of his. Was the story really true? I became a detective and started looking. My curiosity was off the charts. I thought, "If this is true, I have to tell people, because if this is true, it hints at a miracle and a healing process that everybody needs to know." So I became very excited about this.

I did some research and found that, yes, there was a therapist who worked for the Hawaii State Hospital for the mentally ill. Supposedly, he had worked there for four years. Supposedly, within the first two years, using this method, he helped heal most of those inmates, and they started to be released.

Well, I became even more eager to find out this information. It was like, "Who is this guy and where is this guy?" I continued my research until I found him. You can imagine how excited I was. I was like a little kid. It was just joyous to think, "I found this healer, this mystical man, this shaman."

I found him and I sent an e-mail. There was no phone number for him, but I found an e-mail address, and I sent an e-mail to him. He was very kind. He said I could talk to him on the phone, so we set up a time, through e-mail, to talk on the phone. I called him and he was very openhearted and very generous. He spent 45 minutes on the phone with me. I was a nobody to him. He didn't know me at all. He answered all my questions.

I said, "Was it true? Did you work for the hospital for the mentally insane?"

He said, "Yes."

I said, "Did you use some sort of healing method to heal them?"

He said, "Yes."

I said, "Well, what happened? What did you do? What was the method?" I had all these questions.

He offered this confusing statement: "All I did was clean on myself."

I thought, "What does that mean?"

He said, "I worked at that hospital, but I didn't see patients professionally. I agreed to be there but I wanted to look at their charts, not them."

As he would look at their charts, he would feel whatever he felt. He felt anger. He felt frustration. He felt nausea because these were people who had committed violent crimes. They were murderers. They were rapists. These were sad cases.

He would look and he would note what he felt. He would then take what he felt skyward to what he called "the Divine." Some people would call that "God" or "Life" or "Gaia." He called it "the Divine."

He said, "I would take my feeling to the Divine and I would say, 'Please forgive me. I'm sorry. Thank you. I love you.'"

Well, this didn't make any sense to me. I was very kind to him, and I was very curious about him, but I was thinking, "Well, he sounds a little odd to me. This doesn't make sense in the way I understand reality to work."

I kept exploring. I said, "Tell me more. Tell me more about the hospital and what you were doing."

Again, he was very kind and very generous. He said that the hospital was a despicable place. Most of the patients had to be shackled or sedated. When he went there, doctors were quitting after 30 days. Nurses would quit after a week or two. The turnover was atrocious, because the hospital was hell on earth. People would walk down the halls of the hospital with their backs against the wall because they were afraid of being attacked. That's how bad this was.

He agreed to go there if he could do his own brand of healing. Again, I asked him: "What is your own brand of healing?"

He said it was a Hawaiian technique called, "Self I-dentity Ho'oponopono." He said it, and, of course, I couldn't repeat it. I couldn't spell it. I didn't know what he was talking about, but he said, "Oh, it's Self I-dentity Ho'oponopono."

Well, I did my best to stay with him and he continued by saying, "You've heard the statement that you create your own reality." I thought to myself, "Yes, of course. That's in Stage Two." When you are empowered, you know that you create your own reality. That's part of being in Stage Two.

He went on to say, "Well, if you create your own reality, and a mentally ill patient shows up in your experience, didn't you create that person, too?"

I had to stop. I had to take a deep breath. *Oh, my God.* That's a quantum leap in understanding the nature of personal responsibility, because he was saying: If those people showed up in my life, then in some way, shape, or form, I helped create them. I helped create them. This is big, even now, for me to think about.

He went on to say that he was accepting, in some way, that he had created that person in his life. He didn't create that person, per se, but he created the experience of that person in his life. He was taking the feeling that he had, and, looking at their charts, he's angry, frustrated, upset, or whatever it happens to be. He's taking the feeling, *that* feeling.

This is important. He's taking the feeling to the Divine, and he's kind of offering a prayer. He's offering a petition. He's saying to the Divine, "I'm sorry. I have no idea what in me cocreated this person, but I'm accepting that the person is in my life. Please forgive me for whatever I have done in my life, in my past, in my present. I'm not aware of what I did, but please forgive me for that."

He goes on to say, "Thank you. Thank you for taking care of this. Thank you for cleaning this. Thank you for taking care of this whole situation." He ended it by saying, "I love you," which, as I found out, were the three most powerful words you could say. He's saying, "I love you," not to himself, not to the person that he's thinking about, not to his file. He's saying it to the Divine. He's saying it to God. He's saying, "I love you," and by doing so, he's going into a state of surrender.

We Don't Have as Much Control as We Think

This is characteristic of Stage Three, Surrender. I found out from this therapist that we don't have as much control as we think we do.

The therapist's name is Dr. Ihaleakala Hew Len. He has since become a friend of mine. I have done numerous workshops with him. We have now begun to do workshops together. We coauthored a book, called *Zero Limits*, telling the whole story of his mental health years, how he helped those people and how, specifically, by doing this ho'oponopono healing clearing technique, within a few months, those patients who were shackled and sedated didn't have to be shackled or sedated anymore. After about six months, some of them were being released. After about two years, they were almost all released.

This is the most eye-opening, amazing, miraculous story I've ever heard in my life. I'm so blessed to know that I'm the person who has gotten to bring this to you through my books.

Let Go of Ego Consciousness

In Stage Three, you surrender, but why do you surrender? How do you surrender? What do you surrender to? It's very important to understand—and I learned this through my time with Dr. Hew

Len—that most of us are driven by our ego, especially in the first stage when we are victims. Our ego consciousness is all we have at that point. We are being hurt and scared and wounded every time we turn around. Our ego is on red alert at that point.

Even in Stage Two, when we are empowered, our ego is still involved. Many of the intentions we go for and the things we say we want are extensions of our ego. They're not coming from the heart. They're not coming from the Divine. Not for the most part, though there are exceptions.

What I've had to learn in Stage Three is to surrender all of that. When you surrender, you're no longer a victim. You go past empowered into a "cocreating with the Divine" state of empowerment that is off the charts. This is where magic and miracles actually take place.

The Four Phrases

Let's dissect this a little bit. Dr. Hew Len taught me that he said these four phrases: "I'm sorry. Please forgive me. Thank you. I love you." I've since learned that you can say them in any order. I've since learned that saying them silently to the Divine—via your understanding of your connection to the Divine—is the best way to do it. I also know that you can change the phrases. Some people aren't comfortable saying, "I'm sorry." Well, you can say, "I apologize." A new phrase that I've learned recently is to say, "I'm grateful." You can throw in all of these. You can mix them up to make yourself feel empowered by them, or, as in my case, you can actually just say, "I love you."

I have found that if you just say, "I love you" to the Divine, no matter what's going on in your life, you change your relationship to what's going on. "I love you" is probably the most powerful phrase, the most powerful mantra that you can say. I've often asked, in some of my talks, "Can you imagine what the world would look like if everybody were walking around and inside they were saying, 'I love you?' "

What a different self-talk that would create, and what a different vibe that would create, in the world. We're all walking around . . . in fact, I challenge you to begin doing that right now. As you're driving, as you're listening, as you're going about your day, in your head just say, *I love you*. It will make you smile a little bit. There will be a little bit more of a twinkle in your eye. Your energy will go up a little bit and people will look at you, wondering what you're thinking. You don't have to tell them that you're thinking, *I love you*, but you'll change everything around you by doing this.

From Dr. Hew Len, I learned that our ego doesn't have a clue about what's going on. If you're trying to drive your life with your ego, you're going to hit a lot of ditches. You're going to hit a lot of walls. You're going to have accidents. You're going to have problems. Why is that? It is because your ego can see only a small sliver of the world. As I've said earlier, your ego can see only through a peephole into the actual universe. The universe, the Divine, even your unconscious mind, can see the bigger picture.

Ego Intention or Divine Intention?

This is why I tell people that it's fine to have intentions. I've written about intentions in my book *The Attractor Factor*. I've talked about it earlier in this book. Those are good, but there's a difference between an ego intention and a Divine intention. For example, I have said that I like cars. I have a small car collection. That's great, but if I wanted to have the world's largest car collection, one so big that Jay Leno, who is a car collector, would want it or would be jealous of mine, I'd be coming from ego.

If I just allow my goals or intentions to bubble up . . . for example, I attracted one of my cars by being urged from within, intuitively, to check eBay one day. There, about to close in two hours, was an auction for a 1998 Panoz Roadster that was owned by Steven Tyler of Aerosmith. I thought to myself, *I wonder why I just came across this?* I didn't intend it. My ego didn't ask for it. This was not on my to-do list. This was not on my list of goals, but there I was, looking at it. I couldn't help but feel that something within me was nudging me to go in that direction.

Well, I conservatively placed a small bid for it. To my surprise, I won it. I now own a celebrity race car that, as I found out later, is very rare and is worth a lot of money, and because Steven Tyler signed it, it's worth even more than it would have been if Tyler had merely driven it and not signed it.

How did this come about? It did not come from my ego. It came from the Divine working through me. All I did was to say yes to the opportunity when I noticed it. This is an aspect of surrender. It's one of the things I've learned from Dr. Hew Len, who pointed out that your ego doesn't have a real clue what's going on.

An Unconscious Storehouse

In my book, *Zero Limits*, I wrote about some experiments performed by a scientist named Benjamin Libet. These are the most eye-opening tests that you would ever imagine. Benjamin Libet found that when you decide to do something, it is actually triggered in your unconscious mind before it gets to your conscious mind.

In other words, if you reach over to pick up a pencil right now to make a note, the impulse to do that does not start in your conscious mind. It starts in your unconscious mind. It then bubbles up to your conscious mind and you act on it. You feel that you have free will. You feel that you have control over that act, but the reality, based on Libet's scientific experiments, which have been repeated over and over, is that the idea actually comes from somewhere deeper. It comes from your unconscious mind.

Here's another way to look at this: Pause and tell me (or someone sitting near you), or write down, what your next thought will be. You can't do it. You can't do it because the thoughts bubble up unexpectedly. After the thought shows up, you can write it down. You can tell me what the thought was, but you can't predict your next thought. Why not? It is because thoughts are bubbling up from your unconscious mind.

Your unconscious mind is this vast storehouse of memories, of beliefs, of delusions, of experiences, and in Dr. Hew Len's view, even of past lives. He says we have to clean all of that up—that we're actually robots, for the most part, who are just acting on whatever impulse shows up, whether it seems to be a Divine one or an egocentric one. He says that all he's here to do, speaking for himself, is to clean.

When I first talked with Dr. Hew Len on the phone, on that fateful day so many years ago, he said, "All I did with the patients, all I do now, and all I'm doing on the phone with you right now, Joe, is *cleaning*." When I persisted to find out what that meant, he kept saying, "All I'm doing in my head is saying, 'I love you. I'm sorry. Please forgive me. Thank you. I love you. I'm sorry. Please forgive me. Thank you.'"

He was doing that because he was doing his best to clean the unconscious, to clear it of any limitations, any beliefs, any past experiences, any programming that is creating the things he's having in his life. I've learned to do that to the extent that it is my new self-talk.

New Self-Talk

I talked earlier about the self-talk most of us have as being very critical. We're putting ourselves down, or we're complaining about this and moaning about that. Well, my new self-talk is silently in my brain: *I love you. I'm sorry. Please forgive me. Thank you.*

I'm saying that in my mind as I'm writing this to you right now. I'm cleaning the internal part of me as I'm speaking to you.

Why? I'm trying to be as pure a vessel of communication from the Divine to you as I possibly can, knowing that there's a lot of interference, knowing that Joe's personality is here, knowing that Joe has beliefs and limitations and past experiences, all per Dr. Hew Len and his Hawaiian belief that I have a lot of clearing to do. I have a lot of cleaning to do. For Dr. Hew Len, that's all there is—cleaning.

At this point, I've done many workshops with him, and we've done workshops together. We're still doing them together, and I'm still growing. I love being with him because he has this calm vibe. He's just doing his best to stay in the moment, to keep cleaning in the moment, so he can do whatever the Divine asks of him in the moment.

You Are "In" the Problem

Some people will ask questions, and they'll ask pretty much the same questions over and over and over again: How do I remove this person, this thing, this problem from my life? Dr. Hew Len has them look and say something to this effect: "Have you ever noticed, that whenever there's a problem, you are there?" You are there. You are participating in the problem. You don't think you are. Again, that's sliding back into victim consciousness.

It's very possible, through any of these first three stages, to slide in and out of being a victim, or being empowered, or surrendering. You have to be constantly self-alert and self-aware, constantly clearing and cleaning. Dr. Hew Len would answer the question by saying, "Have you ever noticed that you're always there? No matter what the problem is you're complaining about, *you* are there. The one common element that shows up every time you have something to complain about is you."

He goes on to say, "You created it. If you think you created your own reality, this is your reality. You created it."

So, what do you do about it? He says, "Take the feeling. Take the complaint. Don't hold it within. Don't give it to the other person, or the other building, or the other company, or whomever you're complaining about. Take it to the Divine."

Take It to the Divine

Take it to the Divine in a prayerful way. Again, "I'm sorry. I have no idea what, within, me has created this, but here it is, so I must have participated in some way. Please forgive me. Please forgive me because I have been unconscious. I have not known what I have done to make this happen, to create this reality. Thank you. Thank you for my life. Thank you for taking care of this. Thank you for listening to me. Thank you for being the Divine and giving me this miracle of my breathing, living being." And then end with, "I love you."

I firmly believe that if you say "I love you" with total sincerity, and you really feel that the Divine is listening to you, you'll move into this state of rapture. You'll move into this state where tears come to your eyes and you think, "What a great gift to be alive. What a great gift to be here, to be now, to be participating, to be awakening. What a great gift. Thank you. Thank you." You move into this state of gratitude, and maybe you will say, "I am grateful," at that point. When you move into this state of love, you are actually merging with the Divine. If there is any one word to describe the Divine, it is *love*. It is love.

It's Not Your Fault, But . . .

I can talk forever about Dr. Hew Len's Self I-dentity Ho'oponopono and the idea of surrendering, but the one thing that I really want you to understand is that no matter what is going on in your life, you have to take responsibility for it. It's not blame. You're not trying to beat yourself up for it. My favorite way to state this is to say, "It's not your fault, but it is your responsibility."

It's not your fault, but it is your responsibility. The best way to handle it is to surrender. Surrender the problem. Just raise it up to the Divine and say, "I'm sorry. Please forgive me. Thank you. I love you. I'm sorry. Please forgive me. Thank you. I love you. I'm sorry. Please forgive me. Thank you. I love you."

Each Stage Changes Your Perception and How You Play

I love talking about this particular stage, the stage of surrender, but I want to make sure you understand what this is really like. In Stage One, when you feel as though you want to pray for help, you are basically coming from the mind-set of "*God help me, God help me.*" You're begging for help in many ways because you feel like you're a victim. You feel like the world is out to get you. That's one way to know what stage you're in: How are you praying? How are you addressing the Divine, or God, or whatever your concept is of the Supreme Being?

In Stage Two, your prayers may go something like this: "I can do this with or without you." You have a feeling of empowerment, and maybe there's a little bit of ego. You're strutting a little bit. If you talk to God at all, maybe you're saying, "Thank you for what I have," and maybe you're asking for more things. You don't feel so much like a victim, but you're trying to hedge your bet, and you're asking the Divine to help you out.

In Stage Three, your prayer is basically one of surrender. You say, "I can't handle this by myself. I can't resolve this by myself. I could use your help." You're not coming from a victim mentality. You're actually coming from a beloved, heartfelt connection to the Divine itself.

In some ways, you realize that the Divine is in you, and the Divine is in everybody else, and you're making the prayer a request, a petition, to say, "I don't know how to resolve this. I can use your help." You don't hear any desperation in your prayer. You don't hear any desperation in your voice. It's a simple, sincere request for assistance. Also, in this third stage, your prayerful attitude is one of giving up control. That's what surrender is all about. You're giving up your control.

You Can't Control Everything

Let's look at that for a little bit. Why would you want to give up control? It's the idea that you can't control everything. You can't control the universe. You can't control everything in your life. You've already been trying, and if you're honest with yourself, you see that it hasn't totally worked. You have to give up. You have to surrender, but there's nothing negative about that because you still have your ego.

Your ego is going to be with you. Your ego is actually a survival tool. It's to help you drive through the day and not walk into walls, so that you go through the right doors. It's to help you to do what you need to do to have a nice life. I've learned, though, that the ego and your conscious mind can make requests of the universe, with a feeling of surrender, to get even a better life going for you. The problem is, when you try to control, you're coming from your ego, and your ego can't see the big picture of the universe. That's the big concern there.

Follow Your Passion

I also want you to know that when you ask for something, pay attention to whether it's coming from your heart or your head. This is how I knew that it was actually the right thing to do when I bid on the car that had been owned by Steven Tyler—my passion was off the charts. It wasn't just a nice thing, or a heady thing, or an intellectual concept that, "*Oh, if I buy his car, I'll be able to resell it later and make money.*" There was no charge in that. There was no emotion in that. There was no passion in that.

I was looking at it with passion: "Well, I already have a Panoz car, and I know that they're wonderful cars. This one looks fantastic. It looks very rare, and it has been signed by this rock star, Steven Tyler of Aerosmith." My passion was through the roof. My passion, my enthusiasm, my excitement was a real key, a real clue, that the universe, the Divine, was nudging me in that direction.

I have learned in the business world, for example, that a real key to success is to follow your passion. Joseph Campbell said, "Follow your bliss." It's the same thing. Follow your passion. Follow your bliss. Follow your excitement. When you follow that deeper rush of energy within you, it's pointing you in the right direction. It's pointing you toward your path.

This is very important and this is part of surrendering. Again, your ego might say, "Well, it would be wiser if I became a doctor, a lawyer, or an accountant, something in particular," but your divine path, coming from the Divine, might want you to be an artist, a musician, or a plumber. It can be any number of things. I don't want to put a limit on it, and I don't want to judge it. You don't want to judge it, either, because as soon as you start judging it, you're coming from your ego. This is all part of letting go.

"Not My Will, but Thine, Be Done"

I also want to address the idea of feeling bad. Some people hear about surrender, or they've attended a workshop with Dr. Hew Len, or even myself, or they've read *Zero Limits*, and maybe they've had something tragic happen in their lives.

I knew one person whose baby had died, and she looked at this whole aspect of total responsibility and really beat herself up thinking, "Why did she die? I prayed. I did everything. I even did the Dr. Hew Len method, the Ho'oponopono method, and I said 'I love you. I'm sorry. Please forgive me. Thank you.' I wanted that child to live, but the child still died. What was going on?"

As Dr. Hew Len would point out, you were probably praying for the wrong thing.

P.T. Barnum Knew

In this third stage, when you pray, you're basically saying, "Not my will, but thine, be done." This is very powerful. I first came across this when I wrote a book called *There's a Customer Born Every Minute,* about P.T. Barnum, the man who was a circus genius and a marketing genius. When I was doing research on him, I went to where he was buried in Bridgeport, Connecticut.

You have to remember, Barnum was not just a circus promoter. He was an author. He was a speaker. He was an entrepreneur. He was a publicity genius. He was a politician. He was twice elected mayor of Bridgeport, Connecticut. He cared about people and causes. He invented a lot of things that we still use today, coined a lot of terms that we still use today. He was, in all aspects, a marketing business genius.

When I found his tombstone, which was just a small marker on a grassy hill, on it was this phrase, which was his motto: "Not my will, but thine, be done." When I first saw that, I was shocked, because I thought, "Wasn't he an egomaniac who controlled everything around him?"

As I researched and wrote my book, I realized that Barnum, in reality, practiced this spirituality of letting go. He was actually in the Stage Three, where he was awakened to know that he had to surrender.

All the things that he did in the business world, he was doing because his passion drove him there. He knew that the bottom line for him was: If things didn't work out, it was because of a higher reason that he didn't even know at the time.

His museum, which he so loved, the American Museum in downtown New York City, burned to the ground twice. His Iranistan mansion, which was one of the most talked-about mansions on the planet in the 1800s, burned to the ground. His wife preceded him in death, as did a child. In every case, he was able to survive it, accept it, and be at peace with it, because he kept repeating the phrase, "Not my will, but thine, be done."

You Can't Know Everything

As for the woman who had lost her child . . . Dr. Hew Len pointed out that you don't know what the cause is at a deeper level that comes from the Divine. You don't know what is best for everybody involved. What you have to do is to "clean on how you feel." If you're not feeling happy and at peace and trusting right now, in this moment, take what you're feeling, address the Divine, and say, "I'm sorry. Please forgive me. Thank you. I love you."

I know this takes enormous trust, but when you feel as though you can't trust, *that's* when you need to take that feeling and say, "I'm sorry. Please forgive me. Thank you. I love you."

A Practical Tool

I want you to know just how powerful, and even practical, this tool is. This is a way that you can actually improve your business and your bottom line and fatten your wallet and your bank account. For example, I'm also known as an Internet marketer. When I sit down to write an e-mail to send out to my list, to tell them about a new book, a product, a service, a web site, or a seminar, in my mind I'm thinking, *I love you. I'm sorry. Please forgive me. Thank you.*

Trust That It's Working

As I'm writing this, I'm cleaning. I'm cleaning anything within me that I'm conscious of, or unconscious of, that might interfere with getting the results I want. I do have an intention to accomplish something. I do want to send out an e-mail. I do want people to respond to it, but I don't want to control it. All I want to do is trust that it will work out the way it needs to work out. I want the Divine to rule, so I just keep cleaning on all the feelings I have, and I keep infusing my mailings with love.

As it turns out, my mailings seem to do fantastically well. I get excellent results, but it's not just me. When I was first writing my book, *Zero Limits*, my friend Bill Hibbler wanted to test this. He and I wrote a book called *Meet and Grow Rich*. Bill is very intelligent and also very skeptical. He wanted to find out whether he could really improve his results and his sales by just saying, "I love you. I'm sorry. Please forgive me. Thank you."

He put it to a test. He thought of his list, a list of his customers. He just thought of his list. He didn't mail anything to his list. He *thought* of his list. As he was thinking of his list, he was saying, "I love you." He was thinking *I love you* to his list.

If any thoughts came up, such as, "Well, I don't know if they're feeling a thing by me sitting here and not talking to my list directly," or "I don't know if this is actually working and I don't know if Joe is off his rocker. I don't know if this Dr. Hew Len is a crazy, oddball character or what, but I'll just say, 'I love you' to my list." As all these other thoughts came up within him, he would clean on it, and he would just kind of automatically say, "I love you. I'm sorry. Please forgive me. Thank you." Just kind of by rote. "I love you. I'm sorry. Please forgive me. Thank you."

To his amazement, without doing any mailing at all, he sold 41 percent more that month than in the previous month. He also compared the sales figures to the same month from the previous year. For example, if he did the "cleaning" in December, he checked sales against the previous December to see whether there was any surge. There wasn't. The only thing he did differently to get these results was to sit down in front of his computer, talk to the Divine, and think about his list. He radiated love outward. When he had concerns, hesitations, or objections within his mind, he cleaned on them: *I'm sorry. Please forgive me. Thank you. I love you.*

You Can't Argue with Success

This is how profound it is. I know a car salesman in California who is secretly a big fan of this ho'oponopono and the Dr. Hew Len method and of my own work. He will be cleaning when he talks to people who come in to buy a car. There are people who walk in say, "I'm just looking. Don't sell me anything. Don't even give me a brochure. Just looking." He'll say, "Just fine. Okay," and in his mind, he's cleaning.

I've asked him point-blank: "Do you carry on a conversation with them?"

He says, "Yeah. I'll talk to them about the weather, or, if they have questions about the car, I'll answer them, but in my mind all I'm doing is cleaning. *I love you. I'm sorry. Please forgive me. Thank you.*"

This man, who is one of the most laid-back people I know, has broken sales records for that make and model of car. He has sold more of those cars than anybody else in his industry. All he's doing—his secret weapon to bringing in sales—is to say, silently, to everybody he meets, "I'm sorry. I love you. Please forgive me. Thank you." because of this, people feel something when they're around him. People who walk in, who are just looking, sometimes leave having bought two cars (his and hers) when they came in aiming to buy nothing, or possibly, maybe, one car.

Is this practical? Absolutely, yes. It's working on all levels and it's working all the time. Maybe you're listening and you think, "Well, maybe it worked for you. Maybe it worked for him. Maybe it worked for Bill. Maybe it worked for Dr. Hew Len, but that doesn't mean it's going to work for me." Guess what? You clean on that. You take that very feeling. You roll your eyes to the heavens and you say, "I'm sorry. I don't know where that feeling came from. I don't know where my objections and negativity came from. Please forgive me for them. I don't know how that showed up in my life. Thank you for taking care of it. Thank you for listening to me. I love you."

At first, when you say these words, you may not really feel them, but as you continue saying them, especially after you start seeing results from surrendering, from going into this third stage of awakening, you will want to do more, and you will feel the bliss of doing this in this very moment.

No More Worry

A wonderful side benefit from practicing this particular method is that it removes your worry. If you happen to be worried about something (a job interview, a check showing up, what somebody's going to say), you take that very worry, that very concern, and you "ho'oponopono it." Basically, you say, "I love you. I'm sorry. Please forgive me. Thank you."

Again, it sounds so simple, but when you do this, you release the worry. You actually shrug it off. You might sit up straight. You might breathe a little bit differently. You might have a smile on your face. The whole world changes. The reality is, as Mark Twain said, "Most of the things that you worry about never happen."

When you let go of the worry, you give yourself an opening for the Divine to surprise you with something wonderful. I will be talking about this later, but the real thing that you want in your life is actually in this moment. By clearing away everything that takes you from this moment, you realize that now is the true miracle.

List Your Concerns

This is a fun time to go ahead and list everything that might be of concern to you. It can be anything from your job to your relationships to your kids. You might be concerned about your health. You might be concerned about your next mortgage payment or car payment. You might be concerned about the environment. You might be concerned about the political climate. There are all kinds of things that might show up. As you understand by now, if they're showing up in your reality, you've participated, on some level, in creating them.

Make a long list of all of these things. It's a wonderful thing to just dump them on paper. It's very freeing and therapeutic all by itself. I invite you, and even challenge you, to make a complete and exhaustive list. Anything and everything that shows up. Anything that disturbs you. Anything that worries you. Anything that's been on your mind repeatedly that just keeps showing up. Put that down on paper. Put it in your writing. Don't judge it. Don't condemn it. Don't judge yourself. Don't blame yourself. All you're doing is taking an inventory of the things that disturb you at this point. Put those things in writing.

After you've finished writing, I'm going to invite you to clean on one of these items. You can do this repeatedly. You don't need my help to do it, but I'll help you the first time around. Look at your entire list, and if you haven't made the list yet, that's all right, just pick whatever comes to mind right now. Something is no doubt bothering you.

It's pretty much the human condition that there is something on your mind, something that irritates you, something that you would complain about. It's okay to have that. I want you to acknowledge it and I want you to hold onto it for a moment. Pick something, anything, for the purposes of this exercise, and I'm going to walk you through the cleaning experience.

Follow along with me, because for the next 15 or 20 minutes, I'm going to guide you in a clearing process. You can do this with one item or several items. Whatever comes up, go ahead and write it down. You might even keep track of what's going on for the next 30 days. Maybe do this for a couple minutes a day, every day, for 30 days. Write it down and see how your life evolves, how it changes, by just awakening to the stage of surrender.

What I'm going to do first is to ask you to hold onto that feeling and then, second, silently repeat, "I'm sorry. Please forgive me. Thank you. I love you. I'm sorry. Please forgive me. Thank you. I love you."

I'm going to repeat these several times for several minutes. You can say them silently in your mind. You can say them along with me or speed them up if you like. Just allow the feeling that you have to be there as you ask the Divine to let it go.

I'm sorry. Please forgive me. Thank you. I love you.

I'm sorry. Please forgive me. Thank you. I love you.

I'm sorry. Please forgive me. Thank you. I love you.

I'm sorry. Please forgive me. Thank you. I love you.

I'm sorry. Please forgive me. Thank you. I love you.

I'm sorry. Please forgive me. Thank you. I love you.

I'm sorry. Please forgive me. Thank you. I love you.

I'm sorry. Please forgive me. Thank you. I love you.

I'm sorry. Please forgive me. Thank you. I love you.

I'm sorry. Please forgive me. Thank you. I love you.

I'm sorry. Please forgive me. Thank you. I love you.

I'm sorry. Please forgive me. Thank you. I love you.
I'm sorry. Please forgive me. Thank you. I love you.
I'm sorry. Please forgive me. Thank you. I love you.
I'm sorry. Please forgive me. Thank you. I love you.
I'm sorry. Please forgive me. Thank you. I love you.
I'm sorry. Please forgive me. Thank you. I love you.
I'm sorry. Please forgive me. Thank you. I love you.
I'm sorry. Please forgive me. Thank you. I love you.
I'm sorry. Please forgive me. Thank you. I love you.
I'm sorry. Please forgive me. Thank you. I love you.
I'm sorry. Please forgive me. Thank you. I love you.
I'm sorry. Please forgive me. Thank you. I love you.
I'm sorry. Please forgive me. Thank you. I love you.
I'm sorry. Please forgive me. Thank you. I love you.
I'm sorry. Please forgive me. Thank you. I love you.
I'm sorry. Please forgive me. Thank you. I love you.
I'm sorry. Please forgive me. Thank you. I love you.
I'm sorry. Please forgive me. Thank you. I love you.
I'm sorry. Please forgive me. Thank you. I love you.
I'm sorry. Please forgive me. Thank you. I love you.
I'm sorry. Please forgive me. Thank you. I love you.
I'm sorry. Please forgive me. Thank you. I love you.
I'm sorry. Please forgive me. Thank you. I love you.
I'm sorry. Please forgive me. Thank you. I love you.
I'm sorry. Please forgive me. Thank you. I love you.
I'm sorry. Please forgive me. Thank you. I love you.
I'm sorry. Please forgive me. Thank you. I love you.
I'm sorry. Please forgive me. Thank you. I love you.
I'm sorry. Please forgive me. Thank you. I love you.
I'm sorry. Please forgive me. Thank you. I love you.
I'm sorry. Please forgive me. Thank you. I love you.

I'm sorry. Please forgive me. Thank you. I love you.
I'm sorry. Please forgive me. Thank you. I love you.
I'm sorry. Please forgive me. Thank you. I love you.
I'm sorry. Please forgive me. Thank you. I love you.
I'm sorry. Please forgive me. Thank you. I love you.
I'm sorry. Please forgive me. Thank you. I love you.
I'm sorry. Please forgive me. Thank you. I love you.
I'm sorry. Please forgive me. Thank you. I love you.
I'm sorry. Please forgive me. Thank you. I love you.
I'm sorry. Please forgive me. Thank you. I love you.
I'm sorry. Please forgive me. Thank you. I love you.
I'm sorry. Please forgive me. Thank you. I love you.
I'm sorry. Please forgive me. Thank you. I love you.
I'm sorry. Please forgive me. Thank you. I love you.
I'm sorry. Please forgive me. Thank you. I love you.
I'm sorry. Please forgive me. Thank you. I love you.
I'm sorry. Please forgive me. Thank you. I love you.
I'm sorry. Please forgive me. Thank you. I love you.
I'm sorry. Please forgive me. Thank you. I love you.
I'm sorry. Please forgive me. Thank you. I love you.
I'm sorry. Please forgive me. Thank you. I love you.
I'm sorry. Please forgive me. Thank you. I love you.
I'm sorry. Please forgive me. Thank you. I love you.
I'm sorry. Please forgive me. Thank you. I love you.
I'm sorry. Please forgive me. Thank you. I love you.
I'm sorry. Please forgive me. Thank you. I love you.
I'm sorry. Please forgive me. Thank you. I love you.
I'm sorry. Please forgive me. Thank you. I love you.
I'm sorry. Please forgive me. Thank you. I love you.
I'm sorry. Please forgive me. Thank you. I love you.
I'm sorry. Please forgive me. Thank you. I love you.
I'm sorry. Please forgive me. Thank you. I love you.

I'm sorry. Please forgive me. Thank you. I love you.
I'm sorry. Please forgive me. Thank you. I love you.
I'm sorry. Please forgive me. Thank you. I love you.
I'm sorry. Please forgive me. Thank you. I love you.
I'm sorry. Please forgive me. Thank you. I love you.
I'm sorry. Please forgive me. Thank you. I love you.
I'm sorry. Please forgive me. Thank you. I love you.
I'm sorry. Please forgive me. Thank you. I love you.
I'm sorry. Please forgive me. Thank you. I love you.
I'm sorry. Please forgive me. Thank you. I love you.
I'm sorry. Please forgive me. Thank you. I love you.
I'm sorry. Please forgive me. Thank you. I love you.
I'm sorry. Please forgive me. Thank you. I love you.
I'm sorry. Please forgive me. Thank you. I love you.
I'm sorry. Please forgive me. Thank you. I love you.
I'm sorry. Please forgive me. Thank you. I love you.
I'm sorry. Please forgive me. Thank you. I love you.
I'm sorry. Please forgive me. Thank you. I love you.
I'm sorry. Please forgive me. Thank you. I love you.
I'm sorry. Please forgive me. Thank you. I love you.
I'm sorry. Please forgive me. Thank you. I love you.
I'm sorry. Please forgive me. Thank you. I love you.
I'm sorry. Please forgive me. Thank you. I love you.
I'm sorry. Please forgive me. Thank you. I love you.
I'm sorry. Please forgive me. Thank you. I love you.
I'm sorry. Please forgive me. Thank you. I love you.
I'm sorry. Please forgive me. Thank you. I love you.
I'm sorry. Please forgive me. Thank you. I love you.
I'm sorry. Please forgive me. Thank you. I love you.
I'm sorry. Please forgive me. Thank you. I love you.
I'm sorry. Please forgive me. Thank you. I love you.

I'm sorry. Please forgive me. Thank you. I love you.
I'm sorry. Please forgive me. Thank you. I love you.
I'm sorry. Please forgive me. Thank you. I love you.
I'm sorry. Please forgive me. Thank you. I love you.
I'm sorry. Please forgive me. Thank you. I love you.
I'm sorry. Please forgive me. Thank you. I love you.
I'm sorry. Please forgive me. Thank you. I love you.
I'm sorry. Please forgive me. Thank you. I love you.
I'm sorry. Please forgive me. Thank you. I love you.
I'm sorry. Please forgive me. Thank you. I love you.
I'm sorry. Please forgive me. Thank you. I love you.
I'm sorry. Please forgive me. Thank you. I love you.
I'm sorry. Please forgive me. Thank you. I love you.

Chapter 5

Stage Four
Awakening

You can quiet your mind, merge with the Divine, and make a request for something you'd like to have, do, or be.

—Joe Vitale

Welcome to Stage Four, which is the stage where you are awakened. In many ways, this is the most difficult to describe. The earlier stages allow you to awaken into them and transcend them. As you read those earlier chapters, you probably had pops in awareness. You probably transcended some old ways of thinking; but in this stage, you awaken almost by grace.

I want to lead you in that direction so you fully understand what to look for, and I want to guide you into setting up the parameters that actually allow this to happen. Again, this is beyond surrender. This is the stage where you awaken to being the Divine itself. Stay with me, because I know, at first glance, that concept is a little bit confusing and challenging, but let me walk you through it.

The Witness

Right now, as you're reading this, you know you have thoughts. We went through the exercise, in an earlier chapter, where you realized that you're not your thoughts; but let's go past that. You also have a body. Maybe your body feels good. Maybe you like your body. Maybe it's a little achy in some places. Maybe you need to stretch; but notice, you're not your body. You are aware of your body. You are aware of your thoughts; but you're not your thoughts and you're not your body. Also notice that you have feelings. You have emotions: happiness, sadness, anger, rage, uneasiness, whatever it happens to be. You are experiencing them. You aren't them.

In some way, shape, or form, it's almost as though you are inside a suit. Like an astronaut, you, too, have put on some sort of suit, and you're within it. You're looking out through the glasses, through the visor, to see the world.

If you're not your thoughts, and you're not your body, and you're not your emotions, and you're actually something inside of this vehicle that we call a body, what are you? *What are you?* I'm going to venture to say that the witness who is within you is actually God— that the witness who is having the thoughts, having the body, having the emotions, yet who is detached from all of it, is actually God.

God Realization

In many ways, you are the Divine who has come here to experience being a human. You didn't know it, because part of what the Divine set up was this amnesia, so that you didn't know who you were. You were born into the world as a victim, and you learned, because of this book or something else, to be empowered. You learned, because of *The Awakening Course* or something else, to actually surrender; but now you're getting to the good news that you actually set this up to awaken for yourself. The Divine wanted to experience what it's like to be human in order to cycle through all of these stages and get to the other side, where the Divine realizes: *I am God.*

Please understand me when I say that I'm not appealing to your ego. If your ego latches onto this, then you realize you have not detached from it. If you're truly in the stage of awakening, your thoughts, and the thoughts of the Divine, are identical. You clearly understand that what bubbles up is actually coming from the Divine, because you are the Divine.

Beyond Questions

I once asked Dr. Hew Len, the man we talked about earlier, "What about choice? How do you make a decision?"

He said, "If you have a choice, if you have a decision to make, if you can't make up your mind between doing plan A or plan B, or buying something or buying something else, then you aren't clear."

He pointed out that if you actually surrender, if you are awakened, there's no choice whatsoever. Whatever is there for you to do, whatever there is for you to say, you do it and say it without question, because you are one with the very thing that is urging you to share it.

This may seem very "out there." It may seem very confusing, but stay with me and meditate on the following: *"Why do I have thoughts, but I'm not my thoughts? How am I aware of them? What part of me is aware of them? How do I have this body, but I'm not my body? How am I within it? Somehow, I'm a spirit. Somehow, I'm noticing it. I'm feeling it. I'm wearing it. How is it that I have these emotions, but I can be detached from them? I can actually look at them. I can question them."*

If you latch onto these thoughts, you'll feel them, and you can become one with them, but I'm asking you to separate yourself from them, and then realize that you are not your emotions, your body, or your thoughts. You are separate from all of it, but you are this witness.

The Whiteboard

What, exactly, is the witness? In some of the workshops I give—especially the ones with Dr. Hew Len based on the book, *Zero Limits,* which are called "Zero Limits Workshops"—I refer to the witness as, "the source, the whiteboard." I use the term *whiteboard* because, very often, when I have a seminar, I have a great big whiteboard in the front of the room. I erase everything off the whiteboard, point at it, and say, "This is the essence of you."

You and the Divine have no thoughts. You are a plain whiteboard, with nothing written on it at all. As soon as you write something on it, you've separated yourself from the Divine by that remark. If you say, "The Divine is love," you've just made a judgment call about the Divine and put a label on it. You've just judged it. I'm not saying calling it love is right or wrong, bad or indifferent. I'm simply saying as soon as you judge the Divine, as soon as you call it something, describe it, name it, you are now separate from it.

I want you to realize that you're a little like a drop of water from the ocean. You're separate from the ocean, yet you *are* the ocean. If return the drop of water that is you back into the ocean, you merge with it. That's your relationship to the whiteboard. You are separate only as a drop of water is separate from the ocean.

When you meditate, and you look within, and you separate yourself from your thoughts, feelings, and emotions, you start to merge with the whiteboard. You start to merge with the Divine. This is how you can reach the state of awakening, or even enlightenment.

Satori Moments

If you look back over your past lives, maybe you remember, in this life or in another life, having moments of what's called *satori.* A satori moment is one in which you realize, "*I am one with all. I am one with the universe*." In that moment, your identity, your ego, falls away. You're still aware. You still know your name. You still know where you live. You still have all of the personal history that's in your mind, but your attachment to it is gone. It is the moment you realize, "*I am one with the Divine*."

It doesn't mean that you rule the earth. It doesn't mean that you are "the God." You are not the Supreme Being. I told friends one night that in the movie *Groundhog Day,* Bill Murray says he is God. He announces, "I am God."

When somebody questions him, he says, "I am not *the* God. I am *a* God." That's what you are. You are a God.

When you reflect on your life, especially if you've engaged in meditation, if you've done deep work on yourself, if you've had profound moments of silence, you may find that satori; sometimes it happens when you're sitting in nature; sometimes it's happening when you're relaxing by a pool; it happens, sometimes, when you're driving a car. It can happen at any point. This is why I say it often comes by grace, but when you make the moment for it, when you make the opening for it, you may experience, and you may have experienced in the past, those moments of satori.

Make Time Daily for Meditation

What I'm inviting you to do in this fourth stage, where you become awakened, is to make more time to allow that to happen. I'm suggesting that you meditate more. There are numerous scientific studies that reveal all the good reasons for you to meditate. Besides healing your body, reducing stress, balancing your right brain with your left, and giving you deeper states of creativity and awareness, what I'm really interested in is how meditation can lead you back to the Divine—how meditation can actually help you become the Divine.

As I'm describing all of this to you, you probably understand on an intellectual level what I'm talking about. You realize that you have thoughts, yet you're not your thoughts; you have a body, yet you're not your body; you have emotions, yet you're not your emotions. So, you realize that there's something to this. You understand it intellectually, but how do you merge into it? How do you drop your egocentric awareness and just become the Divine, walking through life much like Dr. Hew Len, saying, "without having choice"?

You just realize that this is what the Divine does; in your particular case, and you go and do it, no questioning. You are God. The best way I know of to reach this state is to make time every day to purposefully meditate. You can do it in the morning. You can do it in the afternoon. You can do it in the evening.

Your Whole Life Can Be a Walking Meditation

If you can, consider your whole life a walking meditation, which is actually even better. It's more of a challenge, because as you go through your day, as you drive along, as you go to work, as you encounter other people, as you work anywhere, as you stand in line at the post office, you are realizing, "*I am not my body. I am not my thoughts. I am not my emotions.*" You are detaching to the best of your ability. In that way, the whole experience of living becomes a meditation.

I challenge you to try to be aware 24 hours a day, and I do mean 24 hours a day. You can become aware as you're sleeping, as well, but if all of that seems to be too much of a leap, meditate every day. Make time—10 minutes, 20 minutes, whatever. Many people meditate twice a day, 20 minutes in the morning, 20 minutes in the evening. You do what's possible for you.

At this stage, where you are awakening, you should understand how important this is. It's essential. Just as you brush your teeth every day, just as you do your routines every day, just as you may work out several times a week, it's important for you to meditate every day.

This is essential for you to do, considering the goal, the prize, at the end of the tunnel: to actually merge with the Divine, to drop your concerns, your worries, your beliefs, your programming, to actually be living what the Divine wants you to live—a life of moment-by-moment awe, magic, and miracles beyond description, beyond imagination, beyond belief.

"Meditation Is Not What You Think"

There are different kinds of meditations, and I'm going to lead you through one of them now, but I want you to make an agreement with yourself that every day, every morning, you're going to meditate. That meditation can be as simple as watching your breathing.

One of my favorite funny quotes says, "Meditation is not what you think." I love it, because it means that whatever you think meditation is, you're probably incorrect. It also means that if you're thinking, you're not meditating. Meditation is not what you think. Meditation is behind what you think.

What I do, and urge you to do, is to close your eyes. Watch your breathing. Just pay attention to the breathing going through your nose and out your mouth. As thoughts come by, just note them. Pretend that they are clouds floating by in the sky. You're just curious: "I wonder which one is next." But even when you say, "I wonder which one is next," you're still playing the thought game, so I want you to go beyond that or, more accurately, behind that, because behind that is the blank screen. Behind that is the whiteboard. Behind that is the ocean. Behind that is God. That's what you are.

When you meditate, I'm inviting you, to the best of your ability, to notice and merge with this Divine background—the background that's at the center of your soul. This background is aware of my words. It's aware of what you're thinking and breathing right now. It's aware of everything that's going on around you. I want you to become aware of it and, to the best of your ability, to merge with it. This is how you create a space for an awakening to take place.

Three Ways to Awaken

1. Meditation

There are three ways to awaken that I know of at this point. The first one I've been describing to you: meditating. Again, meditation doesn't have to be a big deal. If you're not an active meditator, don't worry about that. I actually believe in being what I call "a Mystic in the Marketplace." What I mean by that is that you should go about your day, go about your business, go about your life, your relationships—everything—while, to the best of your ability, *being aware.*

What are you being aware of? You're being aware of how you feel, but noticing that you are noticing it; you are not it. You are somehow separate from it. When you have a thought, you're looking at the thought with a curiosity, but noticing it's a thought; it's not you. When your body might have a little twinge in it, for example, you notice, "Oh, my knee has a twinge," but you're separate from the knee. You're separate from the twinge.

In this way, you can walk through your days while actually meditating. You don't have to sit on a rock. You don't have to go to a separate room. You don't have to light candles. All of these are wonderful to do, and if you feel like doing them, then please do them, but if you're very busy—all of us here in the West are, but even if you're in the East and you're busy—you can find time to meditate by letting it be your life itself. You become a living meditator. Invite an awakening into your life.

Keep in mind, if you're actually feeling as though you are way too busy to do this, and you're actually even afraid of the silence, you can do this in baby steps. You can start small. Be aware that if you create distractions, these are distractions from your ego—you want to turn on the TV rather than sitting in silence; you want to read a book rather than sitting in silence; you want to make a phone call rather than sitting in silence. Take note of these distractions.

Again, you don't need to blame yourself. Love yourself. You're doing the best that you can in all situations. If it really does terrify you, the very thought of going to your core and being at peace and being totally silent, you can clean on that by using the clearing technique I talked about in the last chapter, where you say, "I love you. I'm sorry. Please forgive me. Thank you."

I want you to be peaceful with yourself. Be gentle with yourself. It's not going to help if you get rough with yourself, if you put pressure on yourself, if you try to force yourself to do anything.

As we talked about in the last stage, surrender is very important. To surrender to the Divine means that you're trusting that everything is working out for the highest good of all concerned, including yourself. If you don't feel like sitting down to meditate, and if you don't feel like doing some of the active meditations other people have done, treat your life as a meditation. Just gently be aware: "*I'm having thoughts. I'm having feelings. I'm having bodily aches and pains or pleasures.*" Whatever issues you have, become aware of all of those. That's the first way to invite an awakening.

2. Gratitude

The second stage is the extension of something we talked about earlier. The second stage is all about gratitude. I talked about gratitude quite a bit earlier, but you're at a different place at this point. We're now talking about Stage Four—about awakening to the godhood within you and realizing that you are actually merged with the

Divine, that you are an expression of the Divine. The experience of gratitude at this point is going to be very different than it was earlier.

The experience of gratitude is going to be deeper and richer for you, because if you really understand that you are God, that you are the Divine, and that you are here having this wonderful human experience as a spiritual being within a body, then you have a whole lot to be grateful for. I invite you to do something fun to express your gratitude. It could be to write a song or a poem or to create a collage of beautiful photos. Any of these activities might produce feelings of gratitude within you. It could be to give a speech, to write a play, to do something with photography, to do something with art, to do something with dance. In some way, shape, or form, try to give concrete expression to your gratitude.

Something I do, almost daily, is to get into the hot tub at night. As I'm sitting under the Texas sky, I am feeling gratitude. I look up at the stars and, as I look at every star, I say, "I love you. I'm sorry. Please forgive me. Thank you." The stars become triggers for each one of those statements. I'll go through everything I'm grateful for, and I allow those feelings to wash over me: *"Oh, I'm grateful for, well, first thing, the hot tub. That's wonderful. The stars themselves. The sky. My life and how I've transformed it—from being homeless to being whatever I am today. I keep growing, and I keep becoming more and more aware, and I keep welcoming the Divine to come into my life and express itself through me."*

I merge into this state of gratitude so deeply that, believe me, I start to cry. I sit in that hot tub with tears rolling from my eyes, and I'm thinking, *"What an incredible life—to go from this unknown, homeless, unhappy, melancholy, suicidal, even alcoholic fellow to, 30-some years later, creating a course on Awakening, having best-selling books, and being in all these movies."*

I choke up just thinking about it. I do that in my hot tub, and I just feel this overwhelming gratitude. Again, this is available to you. In whatever way, shape, or form it feels like coming through you, I urge you to express it. I urge you to share it. This is a wonderful way to anchor the feeling of gratitude, but because this is the second step to possibly opening you to an awakening, you are setting yourself up to knock on the door of the Divine and say, "Let me in," and, "I am grateful."

Gratitude is such a powerful tool. It not only makes you feel better, but it merges you with the essence of the Divine itself. I think this second step, about feeling gratitude and expressing it in some way, is a powerful one that you can do freely whenever you want to. I urge you to do that—and to do it today.

3. Be Happy Now

The third way that you can invite the awakening to come to you is something really profound. I'll say it briefly: You can be happy right now.

I've given many talks, and in them I've told people that all of your desiring—your quest for a new home, a relationship, better health, more wealth, a new job (fill in the blank, whatever you're chasing)—is, in many ways, an illusion. It's chasing you up trees. It is keeping you busy as you leave this moment, looking down at the moment, thinking, "Oh, when the next moment comes along and I get that car [or that house, or that job, or that relationship—fill in the blank], I will be happy."

That's the great joke. That is the great irony about all of this. You delude yourself. We've all done it. I've done it. We've done it in all the previous stages. We delude ourselves, thinking that when we get the thing we want the most, we will finally and forever be happy—and it doesn't happen.

When you do attract the health, the wealth, the car (or whatever it happens to be), for a moment, you have that thrill. It's the thrill of accomplishment. Your ego is gratified, and maybe even the Divine, working through you, gives you a little wink, as in, "Well done," but suddenly you think, "That's a great car, but there's another one over here that's even better, and faster, and newer, and a different color," or, "I have a nice house, but there's a castle over here that's better and bigger," or, "I have now great wealth coming in, but there's more wealth down the road, and somebody has more money than me," or you have the great health, but you're thinking, "Oh, I'm not Superman [or Superwoman], and I want even more," and suddenly, you're off on the quest again.

Suddenly, you're chasing the dream again, and suddenly, you're no longer in the moment again. What you want is to be happy right now. Well, you can be happy right now. When you attach your happiness to something else, you've separated yourself from this moment. The Divine is *in this moment*. Your power is in this moment. Your happiness is in this moment.

When I say that, I am talking about *this very moment,* not the one that just passed, not the one that's coming up. I'm talking about this very moment—the one where I just said "this" and "this" and "this" and "this." In every one of these moments, you can be happy by choosing to be.

This does not mean that you won't get a new car, or a new house, or a new relationship, or better health, or more wealth, or whatever it is that you're looking for. It doesn't mean that you're not going to take any action. It means that, out of this moment and out of this happiness, the Divine itself will nudge you in the direction of what's right for you. It might be a car, or a house, a relationship, health, or wealth, whatever; but if you can be in this moment and truly look around and say, "Oh, wow," you are manifesting gratitude.

You're looking around this moment and you think, "This is actually pretty good. My moment is actually pretty good. I have worries, but I can clean on the worries and let those go and see behind them—because worries are merely thoughts—to be in this moment." When you're in this moment, all is well.

Another way to find out whether or not you're in the moment is to pay attention to your inner dialogue when you're having a conversation with somebody. Most people aren't paying attention. They're not listening. What they're doing inside themselves is preparing their counterargument, or perhaps they're not listening at all. They have their own story, their own agenda, so they're not in the moment.

Pay attention to see whether that's the case with you. When you have a watercooler conversation, when you go to lunch or dinner, when you talk to somebody on the phone, see whether you're actually paying attention, or whether you're paying attention to what you want to say instead of what the other person is saying. That's a clue that you've left the moment.

As a practice, why don't you start just listening to the person who's speaking to you and trust that, out of the moment, the right thing will come for you to say in return? Don't worry about what you're going to say. Don't stress about what you're going to say. Just take a deep breath and *really listen* to that other person. That will help bring it into the moment, and I also think you're going to have much richer and deeper conversations with this kind of dialogue and listening going on.

So, the third way to open yourself to this awakening is to take a deep breath, and, as you let it out, release everything. Look around you, and maybe touch the dashboard of your car if you're in your car, or the chair if you're sitting in a chair, or the equipment if you're working out—and just kind of rub that object. It helps remind you: "This is my moment. I'm alive. All is well. This is wonderful."

That sense of being in the moment now can open you to a satori moment, if not an outright awakening. That is the third way to open yourself to the fourth stage of awakening today.

Detachment Allows More Richness

If you're concerned about things like nonattachment, and if you're detached from your feelings, your thoughts, and your body, will life become boring? Will life becoming uninteresting? Will you not have pleasures anymore? Will you not have pain anymore? Will you become inhuman in some way, shape, or form? That's a misconception. You're not getting a lobotomy.

When you become awake, you actually enjoy life to its richest, fullest extent. You are coming from the inner sense of peace, and you no longer need outer circumstances to bring you happiness. You're detached from your need, from your addiction, that things must be a certain way. You are free.

Certainly, you enjoy the ups and downs of life, but with a sense of detachment that tells you it's all part of the theater. It's all part of the game. It's all part of the act. You have your role to play. Other people have their roles to play. If we all play our parts, we have this wonderful symphony going on, and everybody is just doing what they're here to do.

Again, you're not getting a lobotomy. You are actually enjoying life; you're actually opening your heart. You're opening your soul, your spirit, your mind to this expanded sense of consciousness where you enjoy the richness of life to a degree that you never could have imagined at any other stage. This is a powerful place to be. It is a glorious place to be. Welcome it. Relish it. Wallow in it. Enjoy it. This is a great time—a great time.

Cues That You're Not in the Moment

Let's look at some cues that reveal when you've left the moment, because I talked about being in the now, and some people may think—or you yourself might think—that you're in the now, but maybe you've deceived yourself. For example, I know a person who keeps a lot of things in his garage. He's just holding on to the past. It's all piled up in there. Another person I know has collected a lot of things to give away in the future, and this, too, is all piled up. It's looking for the future, waiting for the future to happen, before it is released and shared.

Whenever you are afraid or worried, you are coming from the past. You are projecting what happened in the past into the future. That means you're not here in this moment. I mentioned it earlier, but maybe it's worth reiterating: When you actually are in this moment, everything really is okay.

That's one of the most wonderful things, or thoughts, to remind yourself of. If you are concerned, it's because of a thought. You can release the thought, change the thought, or look at the thought and think, "Well, that thought is probably from the past, and the thought is based on something that took place a long time ago, and I'm projecting into the future that it's going to happen again, so I'm worried about it."

If you look past all of that and realize that right now, in this moment, all is well, you've brought yourself back into your power center. Your power center is in your body and your body is in this moment. That's a great way to find out if you've left, mentally, to go into the future or the past.

Daydreaming, for example, could do that. I'm not saying there's anything wrong with daydreaming, because it's useful in earlier stages, but we're talking about *awakening* at this point.

When you're daydreaming, your ego is playing with possibilities of things that might delight you in the future; but if you come back to this moment, and you and the Divine are shaking hands right here, right now, you realize you don't need anything else. You would welcome other experiences, and they will come, and they will be pleasurable, but if you stay in this moment, you find that your daydreams are actually a limitation to what's possible for you. The Divine itself will bring you more than you ever could have daydreamed about, as long as you stay here in the moment where the Divine actually is.

Daydreams Are Like Training Wheels

If you've seen *The Secret,* or you're thinking about earlier stages in this process of awakening, you might be a little confused, because I just said, "Don't daydream," yet the Law of Attraction, Nevillizing your goal, and *The Secret* itself all talk about getting visualizing something you want, especially the end result.

Well, I want to point out that this is useful in earlier stages of enlightenment. When you get to this fourth stage, you don't need that anymore. It's a little bit like being in first grade. You might need particular crayons and particular paper in order to accomplish something, but by the time you're in sixth grade, by the time you've graduated, by the time you're in graduate school, you no longer need those first-grade crayons.

It's a little bit like learning how to ride a bike. When you're a little kid and you first start learning how to ride a bike, you have training wheels on it. You don't really need those training wheels, but because you're just learning how to walk through the world, or in this case, ride a bike through the world, those training wheels really come in handy. After you know how to maintain your balance, how to pedal, and so forth, you take the training wheels off. That's what's going on here.

In Stage Four, you don't need the training wheels. You don't need to be feeling the future and begging the universe to give you something in particular. Those are coming from earlier stages. If you are in the victimhood stage, you might use something like that. In Stage Two, Empowerment, you know about imagery and so forth. But, by the time you get to Stage Three, Surrender, you start to let that go. You start to understand that you are surrendering to the Divine, which knows more, and has more for you, than you could ever imagine.

By the time you get to Stage Four, you're not doing any of those things from the earlier stages, because now you are one with the

Divine. Do you really think God would need to sit down and imagine something with feeling in order for it to happen? That's where you are coming from. *The Secret,* the Law of Attraction, *The Attractor Factor*— these are useful at the earlier stages. You have now transcended that.

Ways to Help You Move through the Four Stages

1. Gather Your Satori Moments

To remind you, the four stages are (1) Victimhood, (2) Empowerment, (3) Surrender, and (4) Awakening.

To help you go through these stages—because you'll probably slide around through them for a little while until you actually lock in and, through grace, awaken—write down your ideas. There's a reason for this. If you remember, earlier I said that you get more of what you focus on.

In your writing, let's focus on some really wonderful moments that you've had that were possibly satori experiences, where you had a peek at the Divine. Maybe it was when you saw a beautiful child smiling at you. Maybe it was in nature and you saw an animal, or a tree, or a leaf floating through the air. Maybe it was at a sports event, where something magical happened at the right moment, and there was an awakening within you. Maybe something you read. Reading can often do that. It has done that for me many times. Maybe it was from an actual meditation. There are lots of different meditations. Maybe you've done something in the past that brought it along. Maybe while reading this very book, you've had an "Aha" moment, or several "Aha" moments.

I'm inviting you to write them down. List them. Describe them. Anchor them. For one thing, you're telling your mind that you want more of this. You are inviting more of this into your experience. Remember, whatever you focus on will expand, so focus on those

"Aha," satori, wonderful experiences, where you felt, at least for a moment, one with all. Do that now.

2. Ask for Help from the Masters

Another thing you can do is ask the great Masters of the world, living and passed on, to open you, to advise you, and to lead you to this state of awakening. I'm talking about Jesus, Buddha, Gandhi, Mother Teresa, and the great Hindu gods and goddesses. There's a whole line of them. You don't need to know them. What you're doing is calling the energy of them.

In the moment, you simply close your eyes and maybe say this prayer, either silently or out loud: "Please, Masters of the world," or say their names if you know them, "please guide me, prepare me, and show me the way to become awakened."

Whatever they say, whatever you feel that they say, whatever the nudges, the symbols, statements you receive, write them down. Maybe reflect on them. Maybe comment on them. But welcome them. This is all part of preparing you for an awakening.

3. List Your Gratitudes

We talked quite a bit about gratitude. Make a list of all the things you're grateful for. If you have created an outward expression of gratitude, through song, poetry, sculpture, or some other effect, you might write about it. Go ahead and anchor the experience of gratitude by putting it in writing.

4. Meditate Daily

Again, I want to remind you to meditate. It's very useful to meditate for 5 or 10 minutes every day. As I've said, you can become a walking meditator as you go about your daily life, becoming aware of your thoughts, your feelings, and your body. You can also find specific times—in increments of 5, 10, 15 minutes, whatever you can do—to meditate.

5. Notice What Is Happening

I invite you to record what happens. How do you feel? Do you notice a decrease in stress? Do you feel happier? Do you feel more creative? Do you seem to have more satori moments, more glimpses of enlightenment? Use your writing as a tool to help you set the stage to become awakened.

Chapter 6

The Awakened Millionaire

You want to become aware of your thoughts, you want to choose your thoughts carefully, and you want to have fun with this, because you are the masterpiece of your own life. You are the Michelangelo of your own life. The David that you are sculpting is you. And you do it with your thoughts.

—Joe Vitale

Introduction for Joe

Peter: Hi, this is Peter Wink, former Vice President of Marketing for Hypnotic Marketing, Inc. I want to welcome you to this special interview segment in *The Awakened Millionaire*. I want to introduce you to a very special guest. He's the author of tons of best-selling books, including *The Key, The Attractor Factor, Zero Limits, There's a Customer Born Every Minute, Hypnotic Writing, Buying Trances, Life's Missing Instruction Manual,* and his latest best seller, *Inspired Marketing*.

He also has produced several audio and DVD programs, including *The Missing Secret, The Power of Outrageous Marketing,* and a brand-new book and program called *The Awakening Course*. He's been interviewed on *Larry King* twice, appeared on *The Big Idea with Donny Deutsch,* starred in the famous movie *The Secret,* as well as *The Opus, The Leap,* and *Try It on Everything*. He even owns one of the most popular web sites on the Internet, www .mrfire.com.

So, without further ado, I want to introduce best-selling author and a man I'm proud to call my friend, Dr. Joe Vitale. Great to have you here, Joe.

Joe: Hi, Peter. How are you doing?

Peter: I am doing wonderful. How about you?

Joe: Doing great. Let's rock and roll.

What Does It Mean to Be an "Awakened Millionaire"?

Peter: All right. Joe, you talk about what you call the *awakened millionaire*. Can you please explain what it means to be an awakened millionaire?

Joe: Well, the short answer is, you're not worried about money. The longer answer is, you're at peace with yourself, you're at peace with your finances, and you're doing something to make a difference in your life, your community, and your world. Really, it's all about being at ease and at peace—clear, clean with money.

Peter: You've written a book called *Adventures Within,* which, by the way, is absolutely phenomenal. In fact, I wish you would promote it more. I'm probably one of the few people who has had a chance to read it cover to cover. You talk about what I can only describe as one of the most incredible journeys through life. Tell about your background and how you went from homeless to a financially independent best-selling author.

Joe's Story: Homeless to Awakened Millionaire

Joe: Peter, how much time do we have here, after all? That's quite a story. I'll give you the *CliffsNotes* version. Born and raised in Ohio. Worked on the railroad most of my life. I escaped Ohio when I was on unemployment, and I went to Texas. But there was a fateful turn where I was unemployed and then became homeless for a while. I used to not talk about it because it was embarrassing and it was traumatic. I did go to Houston, and I was in virtual poverty for about 10 years. I had to do a lot of work on myself. A lot of belief clearing, a lot of self-esteem issues were at stake here. I kept wanting to be an author. I kept focusing on being an author. I had a play produced in 1979. Most people don't know about that. The *Robert Bivins* interview. And it won an award at the University of Houston back at that time period, but I made no money from it and I was back on the streets right after it.

It Didn't Happen Overnight

Joe: I had a lot of disappointments, and as I kept reading books and self-improvement books and working on myself—thank goodness for libraries, where I could go read books like *The Magic of Believing* and *Think and Grow Rich*—I began to have a little turnaround. It didn't happen overnight, Peter. I had to work at this for about 30 years. It wasn't until 1984 that I had my first book published, but even then, I realized that publishers don't know how to market books. I had to actually learn marketing, learn copywriting, learn advertising, learn publicity, because the very first client I had as a marketer was me.

As I made my first book pretty successful in a conservative sort of way, I started getting clients, and I started to become known in Houston. I was doing all right with that, but when the Internet came along, I started to do what I had been doing in Houston on the Internet. That brought me even more clients.

I think a big turning point was when e-books came around, and I give full credit to a fellow named Mark Joyner, who helped me with my first e-book. When I realized how much money e-books could make—and I started making a great deal of money online—I came out with 17 more of them pretty quickly. Along the way, I started to tell the story about me being a spiritual marketer and how I was always using inside-out approaches—not only for marketing, but also for living my life.

Coming Out of the Fear Closet

Joe: I was worried about it. I thought people would make fun of me. I ended up releasing a book called *Spiritual Marketing,* which was my "coming out of the closet," so to speak as, well, I guess we'll call it an *awakened millionaire,* because I was using spiritual principles in business, and it turned out that the business world loved it. That book morphed into *The Attractor Factor,* which became an Amazon best seller, which is the reason I ended up in the movie *The Secret.* From *The Secret,* I ended up on *Larry King* and *Donnie Deutsch,* and then I was in *The Opus, Try It on Everything, The Leap,* and other movies, in addition to doing more TV shows, more books, and on and on and on. That's the long answer.

Then there's the short answer, because everybody asks me, how did you go from being homeless to being a multimillionaire? How do you go from being unknown to being world famous? How do you go from being a nobody to being in several movies and on national TV? Well, it's the persistence of following a dream.

Peter: Interesting. So the overnight success took 30 years.

Joe: When I look at different biographies and I find that people were an "overnight success" and I dissect that, what *looks* like an overnight success often takes 20-some years. I'm a slow learner, so it took me a little longer.

Peter: Where did your awakening come in?

Awakening from Being a Victim

Joe: That's a wonderful question. There have been awakenings all along the course of my life. I've created *The Awakening Course* to help people understand that there are different stages that you go through in life. The one that I was stuck in, which many people are still stuck in, is victimhood. When I was in the streets, I certainly felt like a victim, and when I was in virtual poverty for 10 years in Houston, I certainly felt like a victim, and that's a tough situation to be in because it's you against the world. You really feel like you are alone; you really feel like you are vulnerable; you really feel like you are defenseless; you really feel like you have no hope.

That's a toughie, but I really think that my awakening began with books like *The Magic of Believing* and *Think and Grow Rich* and all the self-help and psychology books I was reading. Because of the public library, I had free access to them. That caused me to awaken to the idea that I could actually have empowerment, that I could actually have more control of my life than I ever did before.

These things affected me, started me on a path. Also, I'm a great believer in coaching. I even started my own Miracles Coaching program because having a coach clearly, definitely was a turning point in my life. I was able to see my own belief system, and then I had somebody who believed in me when I didn't really believe in myself. I really believe that coaching is a bottom-line, definitive, turning-point tool to have in anybody's career, and it certainly was a change for me.

Peter: Listening to you talk, having read your books, reading a lot of stories from other people who say their parents were partly responsible for where they ended up in their life, I'm just curious: When you were growing up, what were some of your thoughts about money, and how did they shape your early life? Did they have an influence?

Joe: Oh, they always have an influence. This is part of what I teach people: that when you're growing up, you're being programmed by your parents, by society, by the school system, by the government, by the media, by religion, all of it. They're not doing it with any sort of negative intention or purpose, but it's happening to you almost unconsciously. It certainly was happening to me as well.

I saw my father being the breadwinner for a family of four. He was the only one working, because that was the mind-set at that time in our history, and he would come home stressed out, angry, in a rage because he wasn't able to pay all the bills. We went through periods when my parents counted how much toilet paper we would use as kids, and I heard conversations indicating that there wasn't enough money and that there would never be enough money. So that became part of my programming.

I'm not unique in this. All of us go through this. You probably went through this. Parents hear about lack and limitation, and it feels very real to them. They pass it on to impressionable children like me, like you, and we take that to our grave, in some cases. Fortunately, there are books, there are audios, there are movies, there are CDs, there are things that help awaken you. That's my purpose today. I'm trying to awaken people to the fact that they can transcend all of the limitations they have, including the kind money programming I (and many others) had as a child.

Peter: I've been fortunate that I've been able to go through kind of a prerelease of your *Awakening Course* and listen to you discuss a really profound topic. In fact, it's one of the most profound topics I've ever heard about. It's about how people get stuck in a victim mentality. Can you describe how people can tell whether they're victims? How did you feel as a victim, and how does that work?

The Signs of Victim Mentality

Joe: Yes, that's a great question. The easiest answer to it is that when something is going wrong in your life, when it feels like it's not going your way, and you have bumps in the road, and there are accidents and problems and debt, who do you blame? Most likely, you blame somebody else. When you're in the victim mentality, you don't take responsibility. You take some action, but you don't take full responsibility. You look around and say, "Oh, it's my neighbor's fault for having this problem; it's the government's fault; it's the president's fault; it's my boss's fault; it's my family's fault; it's the fact that my parents raised me this way. It's their fault."

You look around and you point fingers. When you're doing that, you're playing the victim. You are playing the victim whenever you feel that "they" (whoever *they* are) are out to get you or that they are controlling your well-being, that they are controlling the rules and regulations of your life, that they are controlling the political system. Whenever you say "they" and point, whenever you blame and shift responsibility, then you're clearly in victimhood.

I want to add that virtually all of us are there. We may awaken at some point and go into the second, third, or even the fourth stage, but most of the time, we all play touch and go with victimhood because the mass of humankind seems to feel victimized. We hear it in the media, so it becomes reinforced; we hear it from the government; we hear it no matter where we are. So, it's around; it's all around us.

Peter: If I'm hearing you correctly, and correct me if I'm wrong, you're saying that anytime I blame something outside of myself, I'm into victimhood. I'm acting in a victim mentality.

Joe: Yes, when you're blaming, you are being a victim. What you want to do is take responsibility. I tell people that whatever the problem is, it's not your fault, but it is your responsibility, and that's a big statement, so I'm going to repeat it, because I really want it to be embedded in people's minds: It is not your fault, but it is your responsibility.

Responsibility Leads to Empowerment

Joe: When there is something going wrong and you have a problem of one sort or another, consider that we live in a high-stress time, so you're not to beat yourself up for it, you're not to feel guilty because of it, but it is in your hands, it is in your face, and you have to do something about it. I say, *take responsibility for it.* When you take responsibility, you're not a victim anymore. Now you are empowered. Now you are taking control. Now you are moving forward. That's what you want to do.

Peter: It's interesting, my friend. I've known you for over 10 years, and I've followed your journey. I don't know if anybody knows your journey any better than I do. It's just kind of funny. I remember at one point you were driving a Saturn, then it was a customized BMW, then an exotic Panoz race car. Now you're buying every celebrity car you can get your hands on. It's unbelievable. How did you turn your finances around? Was this some sort of mind shift?

Mind Shifts Begin with a Leap of Faith

Joe: It was a mind shift, but I think it began more with a leap of faith. I remember when I went to buy the Saturn. I had been driving clunkers of cars. The kind of cars where you are nervous it's going to break down. I was feeling like a victim with that car. If it broke down, I would certainly feel like even more of a victim because then I would have to scramble to find the money to repair it. I remember wanting a car that was reliable, and this is useful, because I set an intention. I'm a great believer in setting intentions. I write about it in my book *The Attractor Factor,* which precipitated my role in the movie *The Secret.*

Set an Intention

Joe: So, I set an intention that I wanted to have a car, and I wanted to have a car that was reliable, that was safe, that was inexpensive. I didn't care if it really looked that nice. I did want it to look nice, but that wasn't the top priority. Safety was number one. Reliability was number two, and I started looking around at cars, and I kept seeing write-ups for the new Saturn, which was coming out at that time. This was long ago in Houston. I went to a dealership, and I was nervous when I went there for a couple of reasons.

One was that I had been a car salesman in the past. I knew that at the dealership where I had been, they had trained us to lie to people and to manipulate people, and I hated it. I learned a lot about human psychology. I learned a lot about how traditional used-car dealerships can be, so I was nervous to go to the Saturn dealership. I was also nervous because I didn't have credit and I didn't have money. I went there because I had a coach who encouraged me, a coach who said, "You should go there, go get the kind of car you want—at least try. Go through the motions and see what comes of it."

So, the first thing I did was to set an intention.

Take Inspired Action and Then Let Go

Joe: The second thing I did was to take action. I remember going there, and I saw this car, and it was a beautiful gold Saturn.

It was a sporty Saturn coupe, and I fell in love with it. I wanted to know a couple things. Did it have a cassette player? That was important to me at that point. Again, I'm dating myself, because it had a cassette player in it.

Peter: Not an eight-track?

Joe: No eight-track.

Peter: Okay, cassette, we'll give you that.

Joe: We didn't go that far back to eight-tracks, but we went to a cassette. That was important, because I was always working on myself. Whenever I was driving around, I was listening to cassettes from Nightingale-Conant, from wherever I could get them, so I needed to know that I could listen and program my mind for success. I was working on that.

Well, the car had all of that. I took a deep breath and filled out the forms to see if I could actually qualify for anything—and I did. I filled out the forms. The dealership wanted me to put money down, and I was so nervous and so uncertain that I wouldn't give them a dollar. The salesman said, "Well the car might get sold," and I said, "Okay, fine with me. I'm just going to give you the application. You call me later if I qualify." And I left. I left and went to play music with some friends of mine. I totally forgot about it until later that day, when I got a phone call saying, "You qualified for the car."

I stammered and said, "Are you sure you have the right person? Does it really say Joe Vitale on the application? Does it really say approved?" He said, "Yes." I got the car, which was my first new car ever. I remember thinking as I drove off, "I have the money to make one payment. I don't have enough money to make the second payment." I had something like a four-year loan on that car, as I remember it. So I left.

Look at the principles here. I set an intention to get that car. I was not of the mind-set that I believed I would get it yet, but I had a coach who believed in me, so I set an intention. I followed his encouragement; I took action; I went and did everything they asked me to do, and then I let go. These are all elements of what I teach. And I actually did get the car.

Trust Even If You're Not Quite Ready

Joe: Now, the punch line to this is, every month when the bill would come in, I would look at it and think, "I don't have enough money," yet somehow I always paid it. The mind shift you're talking about in this particular case had a whole lot to do with trust. When I trusted while taking action, things started to work out.

I got tired of that Saturn after a couple of years, so I turned it in for another new Saturn. It was much easier to get a second Saturn, because my credit was good, I already had a Saturn, I was a Saturn customer, and, for the record, Saturn dealers are not like the old used-car dealerships. They are wonderful cars, wonderful people, and wonderful service organizations, but at a certain point, it was time for me to jump forward. The answer to your question: It had a whole lot to do with the intention and trust, even when I felt, internally, I wasn't quite ready.

What Is an Intention?

Peter: Very interesting. You keep using the word *intention*.
Joe: Yes.
Peter: This is really interesting. You and I know what an intention is. We talk about it all the time. I've read about it in all your books, but the current readers probably have no clue what you're talking about. Can you tell the people quickly what an intention is?
Joe: I love intentions, and I love talking about intentions. I turned on *Oprah* one day. I don't watch her all that much, but I caught

her, and this is one of those synchronistic moments when she said, "Intention rules the earth." I like Oprah. She knows exactly what is going on. Intention is a declaration of how you want things to be. It's a little bit like a goal, but it's clearer than a goal. I think goals and goal setting are fine, but they're usually ego-driven. We've talked about it so much its charm has worn off a bit. I talk about intention because it seems so much more powerful than goal setting.

Intentions are stated like this: "I intend to receive $5,000 in unexpected income over the next 30 days." "I intend to sell seven more prospects on my services." "I intend to get 30 more clients in the next six months." "I intend to get my book published." As you can see, there's a lot of energy and a lot of focus here. There's a lot of conviction in your voice when you say *I intend*. When you state an intention like this, you're doing a couple of things.

Align Your Body and Mind in the Same Direction

Joe: The first thing you're doing is, you're realigning your body and mind to go in the same direction. Your body and your mind can go in different directions. We have subpersonalities. Our body may want to do one thing, while our conscious mind may want to do a different thing. And our unconscious mind may want to do still a different thing. I used to describe this by saying that if you walked into the public library and you had no clue what kind of book you were looking for, you would roam all over the place. But if you walked into the public library and said, "I'm looking for Joe Vitale's book *The Key*," you would just go right to that book and right to that section. You would not waste any time and energy. You are clear about your direction; you are clear about your focus; you're clear about your intention.

So, when you state an intention, your conscious, your unconscious, and all of your body systems are going in one direction, and there's something magical that happens. This is something that the awakened millionaire would know. What happens is that you send a signal into the universe, and the universe almost rearranges itself to make your intention come true.

The Universe Responds to Your Clear Signal

Joe: Suddenly, you'll get a phone call from somebody you haven't heard from. Suddenly, you'll meet somebody, a complete stranger, in a coffee shop or a bookstore or at a seminar. You'll get an idea to do something, to open a business, to write a book, to attend a seminar. Who knows what it will be, but your intention will send a signal out into the universe that's on a magnetic level. Some people know about the Law of Attraction, some don't, but the basic idea is, whatever you're feeling on the inside with integrity is actually going to pull the light to it from the outer experience.

So, intention is very powerful. It's working on multiple layers, and I advise people to have intentions every day, if not every hour. For example, people can be reading this and say, "What do I intend to get out of this? What do I want to get from the awakened millionaire?" You set an intention for it, and lo and behold, you will fulfill it, because you've directed your mind to go on a radar alert. Be looking for that. Intention is incredibly powerful.

Check for Limiting Beliefs about Money

Peter: Now I want to go to *The Attractor Factor* for a while, your best-selling book. You talk about there being another way to live financially. It's all centered around your current beliefs about money and how they have to shift if you want long-lasting change. Can you explain how people can tell if they have limiting beliefs about money?

Joe: The easiest way is to ask yourself, do you have money or not? Well, most people will say they don't, and I think the first mind shift they have to make is to realize that they *do* have money. They actually have some money: They have some sort of transportation; they have some sort of home or efficiency that they're living in; they have some sort of roof over their head; they have some sort of clothing; they may or may not have some sort of job or income or unemployment compensation.

All of that counts as money, and if they dismiss it, they're probably coming from a lack and limitation mind-set. They're probably coming from a victim mind-set, whereas the awakened millionaire comes from an abundance mind-set. That person, he or she, will look around and realize, first of all, "I may want more, but I actually have plenty. I may want a bigger car, a better car, a faster car; I may want a bigger or more luxurious house; I may want a more lucrative job; I may want my own business; I may want any number of things," but the awakened millionaire actually realizes, "I'm doing fine. I do have wealth, I am okay," and he or she is grateful for it. Awakened millionaires are happy now, even while wanting more.

Clear Limiting, or Counterbeliefs

Peter: I was reading your book *The Key,* and you spend a great deal of time discussing the concept of clearing. Can you explain what it means to "get clear," and is this part of becoming awakened?

Joe: Well, I love that question, because this is a very important subject, and it's one that I don't think people are talking about.

There are a lot of self-help books, self-help seminars, and all kind of tools and resources available to people, but until they get clear within themselves, they most likely are not going to achieve the dreams they want. Not all of them, at any rate. Some things will be easier, depending on whether they are blocked within or not. This is what you have to get clear or cleaned up.

My best way to explain how this works is ask people to think back to January 1, New Year's Day, and the New Year's resolutions they probably made. Most people do *not* say things like, "I'm going to start shooting heroin tomorrow." Most people set very positive intentions for themselves as New Year's resolutions. They want to go to the gym three times a week; they want to start dating more; they're going to go look for another job; they want to do something that's healthy and positive for themselves.

Well, why don't they continue it? What happens on January 3 or January 7, sometimes the very next day, sometimes the same afternoon? They forget their intentions. Why? On a conscious level, they had very positive intentions. "I'm going to work out more." On the unconscious level, they had positive counterintentions that were preventing them from working out more—and the more powerful operating system in the body is the unconscious mind. When I say you have to "get clear," I mean you have to get clear of the negative beliefs and limitations that are in your unconscious mind.

We've been focusing on money in this interview. A lot of people say that they want more money, and they focus on more money. They set goals for more money. They might even set intentions for more money. Why don't they have more money? Unconsciously, they have counterbeliefs, beliefs such as "money is bad, money is evil; money will make me greedy; rich people are snobs; very wealthy corporations do nothing but hurt humankind."

Beliefs Are Not Facts

Joe: Those are all beliefs; those are all negative beliefs. They are not facts; they are opinions; they are beliefs. They are active beliefs inside of people that prevent money from coming into their lives.

Peter: So, people tend to think that money is the root of evil. They carry that around, and they have to get clear of that notion completely. Is that what you're saying?

Joe: Absolutely. Money in and of itself is neutral; money in and of itself is paper and coin. What I've learned is that money can make a vast, dramatic difference in your life, the life of the people around you, your family and friends, your community, and the world itself. Money is a powerful, useful tool, but *we* give it meaning, and if you think it is evil, if you think it is bad, you're not going to want it. You can consciously say you want it all day long, you can apply for jobs and open new businesses, but you'll still push it away, because you think it's bad. That's what you have to get clear of.

Peter: Can you give an example from your own life of a past belief you had about money? Exactly how did you go about getting rid of that belief? How do you clear a past belief?

Joe: Oh, you want to dig deep?

Peter: Very deep.

Scarcity Is a Victim Belief

Joe: I like this challenge you've laid before me. Okay, well, first of all, most people think that there is a lack of money, that there isn't enough to go around. That's scarcity; that's victim thinking. The awakened millionaire does not have that. The awakened millionaire knows that there's more than enough for everybody.

There's an abundance. For a long time, I was like everybody else, thinking there was a shortage. So, for a very long time, I thought that the more money I spent, the less I would have, and it sure seemed real to me. That's the nature of beliefs. You don't even know it's a belief. It seems like reality. You look around and think, "Well, I just spent this money, so obviously I don't have this money anymore. It's gone." It feels as though that's it, that you've hit a dead end. You think, "That's my reality, that's how it works," but that's a belief.

When I finally stopped, because I had a coach who was encouraging me to stop and look at my beliefs, I looked at that belief and began to question that belief, I realized that it was a judgment about my life and about my income and about money and about wealth. It wasn't necessarily a fact. It seemed like a fact because I believed it. I believed it without question, and that's how most of us operate.

Inquire into Your Beliefs

Joe: We have beliefs we never question, and they appear in our lives as the reality we attract. I finally questioned the premise and asked, "Is it true that the more money I spend the less I have?" Well, at first, I said, yes. That's what it seemed like. Then I probed deeper. I said, "Why do I believe that?" and I thought, "Well, it's always been the case. It's always been the case throughout my past." Every time I spent money, the money was gone. There wasn't anymore, and I said, "Okay, do I believe that the past will equal the future?" Well, that one stopped me, because I realized that a past belief doesn't necessarily have to be a future belief. It could change.

Make a New Choice

Joe: Well, that interrupted my thought pattern. At that point, I had a choice. I looked at it and I thought, "What would I prefer to believe if I could have it any way I want it?" I'm starting to feel empowered now. I'm no longer a victim. If I could have it any way I wanted it, what would I want? I thought, "Well, I would prefer to have the belief that the more money I spend, the more money I receive."

When I wrote that down I thought, "That feels good," and I started to feel it in my body, and I sat up and had more energy and more enthusiasm; and I probably smiled more and my eyes lit up.

Peter: Wait, you say, "The more money I spend, the more I receive." Now that's a tough concept, I think, for people to grasp.

Joe: Yes, it is a tough concept when you still believe that the more money you spend, the less money you have.

Peter: So, that's a limiting belief in itself.

Change the Belief, Change the Reality

Joe: Absolutely. This is one of the most powerful tools right here. People should start listening to the awakened millionaire, because the only thing stopping income from coming to them, the millions, the wealth, whatever, is a belief. That's it. A belief. If you change the belief, you change the reality. If you change your negative beliefs about money, you start to attract money. It's as simple and as profound as that.

Peter: Okay, we're talking about attracting money, but now I'm going to throw a curve ball at you, Mr. Fire.

Joe: Go for it.

The Law of Attraction Is Only a Start

Peter: In the movie *The Secret*, your character makes a really gutsy statement, and I'm going to quote it. I wrote it down so I didn't get it wrong. "Universe likes speed. When opportunity is there, when the impulse is there, when the intuitive nudge from within is there, act. That's your job and that's all you have to do." Can you take a minute and expound on why taking action is so important to becoming an awakened millionaire?

In fact, if I remember correctly, you are the only teacher from *The Secret* who appeared on *Larry King Live* and boldly said, "The Law of Attraction is only the start. There's much more to it." What exactly did you mean?

Joe: Well, I think I meant what I said. First of all, the Law of Attraction is a start. *The Secret,* both the movie and the book, and even my own books like *The Attractor Factor,* simply introduce the idea of the Law of Attraction. They don't explain it in any depth; they don't give you enough clarity for you to be able to go out in the universe and actually work with it. That's why so many people are critical of it.

A lot of people will follow the Law of Attraction as they learned it in *The Attractor Factor* or *The Secret,* book or movie, and they'll get results. But they'll only get results in areas where they are clear, where they don't have counterintentions within them. If they have blocks within them unconsciously, they will try to use the Law of Attraction, *The Attractor Factor,* or *The Secret,* and they'll say it doesn't work.

The reality is, and this is the graduate school level of understanding the Law of Attraction, is that it is working; it's always working, just like the law of gravity. The Law of Attraction is definite. It is a universal law, but it's working on an unconscious level. What you're attracting is based on what you unconsciously believe, not on what you consciously state or consciously believe. That's the big key difference.

Two Parts: Yours and the Universe's

Joe: The other part, the first part that you quoted there, about taking action, that's of fundamental importance. Way too many people are not taking action. They're sitting around, visualizing, meditating, holding their hands and humming, and so forth, and they're visualizing that the new car is going to show up, or that great millions and abundance is going to show up, but then it doesn't show up. It doesn't show up because they didn't do anything. Manifesting anything, becoming an awakened millionaire, or anything else that you want depends on cocreation. You have to do your part. The universe and the rest of the world will do their part if you do your part. That's another element of this.

The Universe Loves Speed

Joe: There's another element. People ask me how I'm so prolific and productive. I have written over 50 books. I have all kinds of articles and DVDs and audios, and I'm in different movies and have many other projects going on and seminars that I'm doing and speaking engagements, and people ask me if I ever sleep. How do I get all this done?

Well, here's a big secret, and the awakened millionaire would know this. When you receive an idea, an idea for a product, for a service, for a business, whatever it happens to be, when you receive it, it's a gift. It is a gift from the Divine. It is a gift from God, if you will. It is a gift from the universe. However you want to attribute it, it's a gift. I treat that with respect. I realize that the gift came to me and that it may have come to a few other people at the same time. That's the way the universe seems to work, and my job is to act on it right then and there to the best of my ability. For two reasons.

The Secret Is to Act Now

Joe: The first is, when an idea comes to you, there's a sense of exuberance that comes with it. You're excited. You're enthusiastic. It's like, "Oh, my goodness, I have an idea." The lightbulb's gone off. You feel the electricity. I want to act right then and there, because I can use that energy to implement the idea. This is a major secret.

What will most people do? They'll write down the idea and say they'll get to it next week, next month, next year; they'll put it in their idea book. Very often, and I would say 99.9 percent of the time, they never get to the idea, and when they do, they no longer have the energy to implement it. It's gone. The energy comes when the idea comes. So, to the best of my ability, I stop and act right then and there.

If You Don't, Someone Else Will

Joe: There's another reason to act now. I've learned that no matter who gave me that gift, the Divine, the universe, my unconscious mind, no matter where that gift came from, it was also sent to at least five or six other people. That's because the universe has learned that not everybody's going to act on the same idea. To hedge its bets, more or less, the universe has given the idea to five or six people, so whoever acts on it first is going to make millions. The awakened millionaire knows you have to take action; you have to take action now; you have to do it right away, because if you don't, somebody else *will*.

That's not bad, because you can be late in the game and still make money from it. However, traditionally, in marketing—and I know a wee bit about marketing—the first one to market is the one who makes the most money and gets the most fame. These are all reasons why it's *cocreation,* and you have to understand the deeper levels of how it works to manifest anything.

The Early Bird Makes the Money

Peter: Well, I wasn't planning on asking you this, but since you brought up the subject, tell people the story about the DVD program somebody asked you about that you were already making in the back of your house. I don't remember all the details. I'm sure you can share it really well. That ties right into the Law of Attraction and making money and how you ended up making a ton of money off this thing: somebody was talking about it, but *you* were doing it. If I remember right, you did it quickly, too. You brought it to market in a matter of hours, a couple of days. Fill us in on that.

Joe: Well, I'm surprised at your memory. You do remember all these things, don't you? First of all, that's absolutely correct. I had an idea for a DVD one time, and I sat down with a friend of mine, and we discussed it and said, "Let's shoot this," and he came over to my house. We went to the backyard and created a DVD called *Subliminal Manifestation,* and that particular recording was called *Attracting Wealth.*

Peter: This was an idea that just came to you out of the blue?

Joe: Absolutely.

Peter: Okay.

Joe: Yes. That's how the ideas come. They come by grace. The muse delivers them, and you say, "Thank you, bring them on."

Peter: The reason I'm emphasizing this is because we all get those ideas. I probably get a hundred of them a day. I don't do anything about it.

Joe: Well, you're missing out on great millions by ignoring them.

Peter: You're not kidding!

Joe: So, yes, I had an idea and I invited a friend to come to the house. We set up a stool in the backyard under some trees on a warm, sunny day in Texas. He put up a video camera and we filmed it. We filmed it in two hours. So, the elapsed time from idea, to him coming to my house, to filming the DVD and beginning to produce the copy for it, to putting up a web site was probably 24 hours.

While we were out there filming it—and this is the punch line you're referring to—somebody else had the same idea. He called me. He called, but he couldn't reach me, because I was in the backyard filming. So, the call went to my voice mail. When I checked my messages, we had finished our product. We had finished the *Subliminal Manifestation Attract Wealth* DVD. What was the call about? A friend had an idea to do a subliminal manifestation DVD about how to attract wealth using hypnosis principles.

Peter: Literally, he called up about what you were doing, and you were already finished with it.

Joe: Absolutely.

Peter: Wow.

Joe: There are a couple of lessons here: First of all, when ideas show up, more than one person gets them. Second, if you drag your feet, somebody else is going to act sooner than you and make money from it. In this particular case, my partner and I were the ones who made money from it.

Awakened Millionaires Run with Their Ideas

Peter: I'm just sitting here amazed. Taking a product to market within 24 hours is remarkable in and of itself. But the whole idea that you had this epiphany and you just went for it, you let go, put out the intention that you were going to sell this thing right away, and you made money. I mean, that ties together everything we're talking about.

Joe: That's my MO. That's how I work these days. When the idea comes, I act very quickly. Since I'm mostly Internet-driven, I can often put up a web site within 24 hours. There have been times when I woke up in the morning, had an idea, wrote the copy for it, put up the web site, and by that evening was telling my list, "Hey, I have a new idea. You can buy it over here."

I've learned that the awakened millionaire is awake to ideas and awake to the fact that you have to take action when those ideas come. These are important elements that most people don't know about, and, if they do, they don't take action, which is another thing the awakened millionaire would know. Take action. You must implement these things in order to attract any abundance into your life.

The Law of Attraction Is Not Enough

Peter: So then, basically, the Law of Attraction, in and of itself, is not enough. You have to take *action*. Basically, are these things that we're attracting to us, or are they already there? Because we're now open, we're letting go, we're putting out the energy, are those things that were already "out there" that we're just awakening to? In other words, we're seeing things for the first time, but they were always there, and it's just we've taken a different view, that we've shifted our minds. Is that basically it?

It's kind of like when somebody asks you to name everything brown in a room, and you wouldn't have noticed those things had somebody not suggested it and you focused on it. Am I attracting it, or was it always there in the first place?

Awakened Millionaires See Opportunities Everywhere

Joe: Boy, that's a fantastic example. You are simply becoming awake to it. It was already there. The awakened millionaire looks around and sees opportunities everywhere.

Peter: So, there are millions of opportunities all around us. They're here. We just have to become tuned in to them.

Joe: Well, actually, if you look really closely, there are billions, but I'm just stretching people to the idea of millions first.

Peter: We're going to get to that question about billionaire versus millionaire. That's coming.

Joe: Good.

Your Wealth Is Hiding under Your Fear

Peter: One of the things I'm really fascinated about when it comes to you—you're a multifaceted guy. You're into marketing; you're into spirituality; you're into cars. All different things. I wonder if you would share how inspired action made you a marketing genius and a best-selling author at the same time. Your story about how you bridged that gap is incredible. A lot of people look at Joe Vitale and say, "Oh, he's a marketing guy." Some people say, "He's the Law of Attraction guru." But you had to become a marketing genius to get your books on spirituality out there.

You were spiritual first, but you took this incredibly inspired action to bridge the gap so you can get your word out there. Can you just expound for a minute or two on that process, what you were thinking back when you had your first book that you couldn't sell? Where was that shift? You weren't a marketing guy then, right?

Joe: I think the biggest answer that you're looking for here that would be the one that people can chew on the most is that I faced my fears. I faced my fears. I ended up telling people that the wealth you seek is most likely sitting under whatever it is you fear to do. I have to repeat that, because this is amazing. It's profound. *The wealth you are seeking right now, the millions you're seeking, whatever wealth amount you are seeking, it's hiding under what you are afraid to do.* That is profound.

I'll give you a quick example. I mentioned earlier that one of my books was *Spiritual Marketing,* later to become *The Attractor Factor.* I wrote *Spiritual Marketing* as a blend of my spiritual and miracle principles. It was an introduction to the five-step process for attracting whatever you want—and I wrote it only for my sister.

Why did I write it only for her? I'm very close to my sister. She had been on welfare, her kids were ill, and her husband wasn't working. I just felt bad for her. She lived 2,000 miles away. I couldn't see her regularly. I thought, "Let me go ahead and write this booklet and send it to her." So I did. I wrote it, I sent it to her, and it made a difference. She got off welfare; her husband has work; her kids have all graduated from high school and have gone on to college. She's doing very well at this point.

Over time, I gave my booklet to one or two people here and there, whenever I felt safe. Why did I do this only when I felt safe? It's because I was representing the American Management Association and the American Marketing Association, and Nightingale-Conant had produced one of my programs. I was afraid. I was nervous about what they would think. I was nervous about my own mailing list. What would my customers and clients think of me if I came out with a book called *Spiritual Marketing*? They'd be wondering about me, talking about the metaphysical world rather than the marketing world. Or perhaps some would appreciate my talking about the mystical world, but hate my talking about the marketing world. It seemed like a lose-lose proposition.

However, I finally faced my fears, thanks to Bob Proctor, who embarrassed me in front of 250 people at one of his events when he held up my book said, "Joe has written *Spiritual Marketing,* and you're all going to want it." I realized that they *did* want it. Those people mobbed me. They wanted it. I quickly got the book into print, and it quickly became an Amazon best seller, twice. The *New York Times* wrote about that book. *Spiritual Marketing* later became *The Attractor Factor* when a major publisher picked it up and changed the title. By facing my fears, a whole new career opened for me.

Because of *Spiritual Marketing,* which became *The Attractor Factor*, I garnered a role in *The Secret* and all those other movies. So many opportunities fell in line, but they would not have happened if I had sat in a corner with a blanket over me saying, "I am just a marketing person. I can never tell people what I really like to do, which is spiritual marketing. I can never tell them about being an awakened millionaire, because what about the repercussions of it?" I was afraid. When I finally faced my fears, that's when the money came in. That's when the abundance came in. That's when the fame and fortune came in. Face your fears and you will attract wealth.

Apply the Five *Attractor Factor* Steps to Money Problems

Peter: If someone's having serious money problems, what is the first thing they should do, and why?

Joe: Well, the first thing is to set an intention for the money that they want, and they should be as specific as possible. I heard recently about a billionaire who made a ton of money by, first of all, setting an intention for what he wanted—but just saying *money* wasn't clear enough. He wanted money, but that's not specific. He looked at the Forbes 500 list of wealthy people, then he looked at the person rated number 500, saw how much that person made, and said, "All I have to do is make $1 more than that person and I will be on the Forbes 500."

Setting a very clear, definite, concrete, measurable intention is the first thing to do. The second thing to do is to notice what comes up. In other words, it may come up as, "How is that possible?" "How do I do it?" "Do I deserve this kind of wealth?" "Will this wealth actually hurt me?" All of these are beliefs, and these and any other beliefs that come up all have to be clear. I talk about this in *The Awakening Course,* that clearing is the number one thing you have to do. Sometimes you need a Miracles Coach to do it, sometimes you can do it on your own, but you have to look at your beliefs and release them to become the awakened millionaire.

The third thing you have to do is take action. We've talked about this. You have to take action when an idea comes up; when you have the impulse to do something, *act*. Act fearlessly, because wherever the fear is, as we mentioned, that's probably where your wealth is.

The Power of Coaching

Peter: Joe, I want to shift gears for a second. I know you're a big fan of coaching. You run your own Miracles Coaching organization, teaching people how to attract money and attract miracles in their lives. Can you elaborate a little on how you've used coaching in your life? Why you recommend it so strongly?

Joe: Coaching is the single most powerful thing I can think of that has helped me transform my life. I talk about it in my book *The Attractor Factor.* I had a coach for about 10 years who I would see on a regular basis, and this man single-handedly helped me find my beliefs, release my beliefs, and change my beliefs. That helped me go through things like the poverty I was going through. I went from poverty to having money to being very successful. That was because I had somebody who believed in me, somebody who encouraged me, somebody who held me accountable, somebody who didn't judge me, somebody who loved me even as we looked for the beliefs that were holding me back.

This was so successful that, at a later time, when I met a group of coaches who were already working with one of my programs, the Executive Mentoring coaching program, they asked me if I'd like to have another program and I said, "Yes, I've always wanted a Miracles Coaching program." These Miracles Coaches would have to be people trained by me; because, after 10 years of working with my own coach, I knew what to ask, and I knew what the mind-set for coaches had to be. I knew how often people had to meet, so I set up the Miracles Coaching program to help others, just as my coach was the first one who helped me. Having a Miracles Coach in my life is clearly where the credit has to go for helping me get clear to become an awakened millionaire.

Welcoming Money into Your Life Is Key

Peter: How important is positive thinking to becoming wealthy? Can I be a negative thinker and still become an awakened millionaire? You hear a lot about positive thinking, but I know a lot of people who become wealthy who are negative and complaining and everything else. Can you expound for a minute or two on that?

Joe: That's actually a very curious question, and it opens up this dialogue. The truth is, you *can* become a multimillionaire with any sort of mind-set belief system, positive or negative, that you like. It's all a question of, "Do you welcome money into your life?" If you welcome money into your life, then you can be very negative and still attract money. You can be very positive and still attract money. I think you will be a happier, healthier, more balanced human being and a more positive contributor to the world if you have a positive mind-set and are positive about your life and your contributions. This illustrates something very important: Whether you associate money with evil or with good, you're actually wrong on both counts, because you can have any mind-set you want, as long as you are clear that you welcome money into your life. You can have money in your life no matter what your belief system or personality happens to be.

Giving Opens Your Heart to Receive, and Giving Is Essential to Attracting Money

Peter: How important is giving?

Joe: I think giving is a secret to attracting great wealth. People have talked about this in religions. For example, some religions ask you to give 10 percent of your income. When I first heard of this, I was very skeptical, because I thought it meant giving 10 percent to the religious organization that set the rule. But the reality is, if you give 10 percent or more of your money to *wherever you have received spiritual nourishment,* to wherever you have received inspiration—it might be a church, a waitperson, a cab-driver, somebody on the street, anybody—then you are opening your heart to receive.

Giving Is Tied to Your Beliefs

Joe: See, when people don't give, they're coming from a scarcity mind-set. They think that there's only so much money available, and they're going to hold onto it. But, when you give, you send a signal to your own mind that you have more than enough. Then this karmic marketing principle kicks in—that when you give, somehow, someway, the universe will bestow on you 10 times more.

The only thing that I would say as a qualifier or a disclaimer is that, if you don't believe in giving, you can actually interrupt the process. If you want to prove me wrong, for example, by saying, "Oh, that Joe Vitale talked about giving, so I'm going to give $10 to this person and look for $100, but I don't believe it's going to come," then it probably *won't* come, because that's free will, and your belief system can interrupt the universal principles.

I urge you to look at your beliefs in regard to giving. Giving, to me, feels wonderful, which is another secret to attracting millions. When you feel good, you start to attract people and things and opportunities that can help you make more money. Again, giving is essential to attracting money.

Awakened Millionaires Walk in Gratitude

Peter: I know you talk a lot about gratitude and being grateful for everything you have to get more in your life. You talk about that in pretty much all of your books. Can you just expound for a minute on the "attitude of gratitude," so to speak?

Joe: Well, that's another secret for attracting money. When you feel grateful for what you already have, you may want more, but if you look around and say, "I'm grateful for this audio," "I'm grateful for this book," "I'm grateful for whatever is in my life right now," and you sincerely feel grateful, you transform your state of being and send out a different energy, an energy of gratitude. That energy will attract more people, places, and things, more moments that will be even better than the one you have.

They'll all be based on gratitude; they'll all be based on love, respect, and appreciation.

Gratitude is a powerful tool for becoming an awakened millionaire, and, in fact, awakened millionaires walk the earth in gratitude because they know that they're living a miracle. It's a miracle to be alive. So, yes, gratitude is profound, very profound.

Awakened Millionaire or Billionaire? Your Financial Set Point

Peter: We alluded to it a little bit earlier, but I want to go back to the different thought patterns of someone has who is an awakened millionaire versus someone who is an awakened billionaire. How does that work? How does somebody become a Bill Gates versus somebody who's earning a nice seven-figure income?

Joe: Well, that's a great question. What you have to do is raise your level of deservedness. Everybody has a wealth set point within them. Right now, it probably seems possible to become a millionaire but not a billionaire. Why?

Well, the difference is probably internal. At one point, when I was making minimum wage, doing odd little labor jobs, my mind-set, my wealth point, my level of deservedness said that's all I could have, that's all I deserved. Certainly I wanted more. I might even have intended more, but because my belief system said that's all I could have, that's all I had.

I think that each person has to take a deep breath and say, "What do I believe about money? What do I believe about what I deserve?" Maybe you even need to make the jump and mentally ask yourself, "If I had $1 billion, what would my life be like?" My guess is that fear would come up. You would probably think, "Oh, I'd have a giant corporation; I'd need a bunch of accountants; I'd have a lot of tax issues to wrestle with," and suddenly, becoming a multibillionaire becomes unpleasant.

You need to examine all of those thoughts and beliefs that come up with the image. You clear them by saying things like, "Well, if I had a corporation, I'd hire the right people to take care of it. If I had tax issues, I'd hire corporate attorneys, tax attorneys, to take care of them."

As you dissolve your negativity and your beliefs about becoming a multibillionaire, you can then go in that direction. What you've done is raised your level of deservedness. You've raised your set point.

Spiritual versus Material

Peter: There's a lot said in the spiritual community about simplic- ity, about simplifying your life. Things like cars and homes. We shouldn't want for those. There's something intermittently wrong with that. In your opinion, is it okay to have material wants?

Joe: Absolutely. In fact, the way I look at it is that the spiritual and material are two sides of the same coin. Anybody who frowns on money or cars or houses or great wealth is coming from a self- righteous view that the world has to work in what they deter- mine to be a spiritual place. Who's to say that a car isn't spiritual? I actually believe that balanced people have both the spiritual and the material integrated within them.

I don't think there's anything wrong with having cars or houses. I think the only problem might be if somebody goes too much into an ego trip and sets ego-based intentions. I talk about this in *The Awakening Course* and in my Miracles Coaching program.

The short answer is, if I wanted to have the largest car col- lection in the world, I'd probably be coming from ego, but if

I occasionally see a car that makes my heart sing, that puts a spring in my step, that makes me feel good to be alive, and it feels like it's coming from my intuition or a nudge within saying, "That would be wonderful to have," then I think it's probably divinely guided. Who, other than me, is to say whether that's true for me or not? That would be self-righteous judgment. As I said, the spiritual and the material are the same thing.

Awakened Millionaires Never Stop Growing

Peter: Thanks, Joe. I have a couple of last questions before we wrap it up. A biggie that comes to mind. It seems as though the wealthier my friends are, the more they're into self-education and reading books and listening to tapes and what have you. I'm just curious, what's your take on that? I mean, you're obviously very wealthy, but you still read books and go to seminars. How important is education to keeping that process going?

Joe: Wow, that's a great observation, because I am still learning and still growing. Yes, I read books. Amazon is my favorite place to shop, and I'm always getting new books on marketing, psychology, success, mind-sets. I just keep growing and learning and stretching. I go to others' seminars. A friend of mine once said that all the self-help gurus are buying all the other self-help gurus' materials. Why is that? Because we are all growing, we are all moving forward.

I think if you want to have great leaps in your life and jump into becoming the awakened millionaire or the awakened billionaire, it's essential to keep growing and stretching through books and audios and coaching and seminars. Any and all of this, I think, is essential.

Peter: To close, is there anything else you would like to offer about becoming an awakened millionaire—or anything else?

Dare Something Worthy

Joe: Well, you know, on my business card I quote a sixteenth-century Latin motto, *Aude aliquid dignum,* which means, "Dare something worthy." I would like to challenge everybody who reads this book to set an intention to become a millionaire or multimillionaire or, if they feel comfortable with it, a billionaire. I challenge them to start taking action to make it so. I challenge them to work on themselves and on their beliefs. I challenge them to create or find a support system, because having people to encourage you and keep you accountable, I think, is another key ingredient to becoming an awakened millionaire. I challenge people to realize that what they want is to be happy. They can be happy *now,* as they pursue the millions they seek. I challenge everybody to *dare something worthy.*

Peter: Joe, if people want to contact you or sign up for your newsletter, where should they go?

Joe: My main web site is www.joevitale.com, and my Miracles Coaching program is www.miraclescoaching.com.

Peter: It's been an honor and pleasure to be with you here, Joe. Thanks for taking the time and sharing your wisdom.

Joe: Thank you, Peter, and Godspeed to all of you.

Peter: To all the readers out there, thanks for joining us.

Chapter 7

The Awakened Relationship

Once you experience forgiveness, your outer world changes.

—Joe Vitale

Joe: Hi. This is Dr. Joe Vitale. Welcome to the *Awakened Relationship* program. In this program I'm going to discuss how to get the most from your personal and business relationships. Let's jump right in so you, too, can have an awakened relationship.

Theresa Pushkar: Joe, would you describe what an *awakened relationship* is?

An Awakened Relationship Is Love

Joe: An awakened relationship is completely based on love. You have to understand that there are at least four stages of awakening. In the first, most people are victims, and that relationship is not very healthy. In the second stage of awakening, they feel empowered. A relationship can be very strong and very challenging and very growth-oriented because of this empowerment. But sooner or later it evolves into the third stage, which is about surrender. You're not surrendering to the other person in that relationship;

you're surrendering to what I call "the Divine." You're surrendering to a higher power.

In the fourth stage, which is where you and I are headed, you are awake. In an awakened relationship, you are coming from love. You *are*, in fact, love, and the other person is coming from love and is, in fact, love. In an awakened relationship when you look at the other person, you see only love. And if that person is coming from an awakened relationship, he or she looks at you and sees only love, too. Love is the nature and the description of an awakened relationship.

Real Friends

Theresa Pushkar: Speaking of love, do most people have what we would consider real friends? True friends? What in the world is a true friend?

Joe: I don't think most people have true friends. That might seem sad. It might seem startling. But, here's one definition of a true friend, and I heard this from a famous speaker: If you were in some crazed situation, locked in a prison in some Third World country, which of your friends would run to the rescue? Which of them would stop everything, go to the other side of the world, if needed, and break you out? Set you free? When you use that kind of a definition, most of us don't have a true friend. We have acquaintances. We have coworkers. We have neighbors.

We have people whom we see from time to time. We have people whom we like hanging around with. But having somebody who has your utmost well-being in mind, including your entire life in mind, is probably rare. However, when you come from an awakened relationship, you tend to come from love within you, and from that perspective, you attract to you loving friends. A real friend, in my opinion, is somebody who is totally supporting you, your well-being, your life goals, and who has your highest and best interests in mind. And you have theirs in mind as well.

Relationships Are Mirrors

Theresa Pushkar: Joe, we're talking about love and relationships and those who care about us and those who are our true friends, but what about negative people? What about whiny people? What about a life partner who's complaining and whining and negative? What do you do about that? How do you deal with that?

Joe: Well, you know, depending on what stage of awakening you are in, you will at times pull into your life, negative, whiny, and sometimes victim-oriented life partners. This is only because they are representing a part of you. In Jungian psychology understanding, they are the shadow side of you. Now, if you've never heard this before, it's going to be very confusing to hear for the first time. It's the idea that the other person you're complaining about, the negative person, the whiny person, the person you think is acting like a victim, is actually representing a part of you that feels the same way.

So, in a very real way, the relationship you attracted is a relationship that is within you. The first way to heal this is to actually heal your own relationship with yourself. You have to take complete responsibility and look at the negative, the whiny, the victim, as representing a mind-set within you. As you own it, as you release it, and as you become more awakened and more empowered, the other person will either change or leave, because the energy within you is no longer attracting them.

Mutually Beneficial

Theresa Pushkar: I've known friends who remind me of a yin yang situation, where they just seem like polar opposites when they first come together, and then I seem to notice a mutually beneficial situation arriving, where they complement one another in strange and different ways. Do relationships have to be mutually beneficial to last?

Joe: Relationships are always mutually beneficial or they end. If you are not getting something from the other person and that person isn't getting something from you, the party's over. Sometimes, relationships may start a little bumpy, and as they get to know each other and clean up their unconscious beliefs about relationships and love and deservedness, things smooth out. Generally, they'll stay together and have a nice time together. But if at any point, at any time, either person feels they're not getting any more benefit, they will most likely stop the music and move on.

The Key to a Lasting, Intimate Relationship

Theresa Pushkar: Is there a key to creating a lasting, intimate relationship?

Joe: The key to having a lasting, intimate relationship is, again, based on love. What is love? Love is the mutual understanding, the total nonjudgmental acceptance of the other person and yourself. Love has no bounds. Love has no judgment. Love is coming from clarity, from light, from peace, from happiness. In order to have this ideal relationship, whether at work or at home, you have to see the love in the other person. You have to see the love within you. An awakened relationship, again, is based on, and is, love.

Ruthless Honesty—No Secrets

Theresa Pushkar: Should complete honesty be a part of that love? We all seem to have little secrets, little thoughts, little things we withhold from the other person in a relationship. Is that good, or is that bad? What is that?

Joe: Sigmund Freud said the number one way to stay mentally healthy is to have no secrets. I think there's a profound truth in that. I think there's a profound healing that comes from having no secrets. I believe being completely honest with the other person and, more important, with yourself, is the number one key to having an awakened relationship in your life in any and all areas.

It may be uncomfortable, but a long time ago a book was written about "ruthless honesty," the premise of which was that when people are ruthlessly honest with themselves about their past, about forgiveness, about what they want, they bring peace into their lives and into their relationships. Having no secrets is a key, a direct path to the awakened relationship.

Working Together—Personality and Soul

Theresa Pushkar: Joe, I struggle in my personality self, which seems to have so much catching up to do. It doesn't seem to ever be parallel to my soul self, and it's very discouraging. How can I find peace in this discrepancy?

Joe: Well, that's a great question. First of all, you want to accept wherever you are. Because when you fight with it, you make it worse. Resistance will just make it persist. As much as possible, you want to focus on the moment, focus on being in the here and now, and actually focus on what you are calling your *soul*. Your personality self, your ego self will never, ever catch up to your soul self. It's not supposed to. It's actually supposed to be in service of the Divine part of you, which is what you're calling your soul.

Just take a deep breath and surrender to that. Maybe meditate on the fact that you are not your ego. You are not your thoughts. You are not your body. You are not your emotions. You are actually the soul, the witness behind all of it. Breathe into that and realize that the Divine will speak to you in your personality self, and you should simply follow what the Divine says.

When you try to lead from the ego perspective, you're actually causing a lot of frustration, and that's what you're feeling right now. I would let go of that. Let go of that completely. Just look within and follow the Divine. That's leading you home. That's leading you to an awakening.

The Ego Is Your Friend

Theresa Pushkar: That brings to mind another issue. A lot of spiritual teachers describe the ego almost as though it is the enemy, something we want to annihilate. That it's negative. And what comes up for me is that negativity creates resistance or some kind of wall. And, you know, you hear that common phrase, "You have to embrace the ego." It's a real struggle. Can you provide me with some clarity on that?

Joe: The ego is your friend. That's the best way I can sum it up. Your ego is here to help you survive. None of us are here without an ego. An ego is perfectly fine to have. You just don't want your ego to be in control, to be driving the bus of your life, because it's going to hit walls and it's going to hit other buses. It's going to have accidents. So, your ego is not to be demolished.

You need it to get through life. You need it to be able to cash a check. You need it to be able to drive your car. It's your friend. That's really the bottom line here. It's simply that, and I keep repeating this, but it's so essential: The ego needs to be in service of the Divine. The Divine is the one driving the bus. Driving the ship. Driving the planet. And you simply want to be a servant to it.

Children Show Us the Way

Theresa Pushkar: Speaking of driving the bus, I'm thinking of children. I'm thinking of young children, who don't seem to have a heck of a lot of ego, and we seem to train them into ego. Is there a way that your message can be conveyed to our children?

Joe: I actually think it's the other way around. I actually think the children are the purest, most divine little beings among us. They're closer to source. They just came out of being at source. Therefore, they are learning to have an ego. They are learning how to survive in life. We probably need to sit and study them and see how they play, how they interact. See the light that's still on in their eyes. See how their heart says, "Let's go do this. Let's go play with this. Let's go make a peanut butter and jelly sandwich out of the dog. Let's go do something that's fun," because they're simply being creative.

Instead of trying to change the children, we should be studying them and saying, "What qualities do these Divine little beings have that we can adapt and bring into our lives right now as adults?"

Theresa Pushkar: I guess you're also saying that we have to kind of separate ourselves and not attach ourselves to "protecting" our children.

We Can Help Them Be Aware

Joe: Well, I do think we need to protect our children, because they came into the world with a little bit of a victim consciousness;

they're taking on our programming and the culture's programming, and we need to tell them what a bus is, what a train is, what a car is, what a dangerous area might be. Just to help them be aware. We are training their egos. Again, we all have egos, but those are necessary for survival.

A little child doesn't quite have all of those survival skills and social skills. So I don't think there is anything wrong with trying to lend a hand and teach them and prepare them and lead and educate them.

Theresa Pushkar: Sometimes I find it's difficult to discern my fears. You know, for example, even the children. I can get caught up in "Oh my God, I'm going to take her to the schoolyard," and I'm terrified that she's going to hurt herself on the monkey bars. And I'm trying to discern a sense of knowing, or that intuitive, from the sense of fear. Is there a way that I can easily discern one from the other?

Focus on What You Want for Your Child

Joe: Well, it sounds like you're pretty clear about what fear is. I would focus more on what you want. When you focus on fear, you're going to attract more fear. You attract more fear. Your conscious thought—you attract more fear of feelings within you. And you can attract more fearful experiences because of where you began with this.

Take a deep breath and focus on, "What do I want? I want my child or myself to be safe and playful and inspiring and inspired. I want to be able to take her or him to the playground and have fun there. I want to be able to smile and talk to the other people and see my child play with the other kids." I would focus on just how good that feels.

When you focus on what you want, you tend to expand that and attract that. This is a basic rule of psychology. I've said it before in *The Awakening Course*. You get more of whatever you focus on. So focus on what you want, not on what you're worried about. Whatever you focus on, you'll attract.

Fear Just Means You Haven't Done It Before

Theresa Pushkar: Well, taking that jump into business, there's some huge decisions we have to make, and many of us tend to be very risk-averse. There can be a sense of, "I better not do this; it could be dangerous," and it's hard at times to distinguish that intuitive gut feeling from one of, "I am just so in fear, because this could be a huge change or shift in my life."

Joe: Here's that subject of fear again. Doesn't it show up about everywhere? Isn't that interesting? I would say that fear is coming from that first stage of being a victim. We are afraid because we're afraid we're going to get hurt, we're going to lose money, we're going to lose face, we're going to lose our investments, we're not going to be proud of ourselves. This is a great joke, too, because I've learned from a billionaire, a guy who had failed many times, had declared bankruptcy at one point and is now a billionaire, who told me, "I learned something great from fear and from failure," and I said, "Well, what in the world was that?" He said, "When you fail, nothing bad happens to you." Nothing bad happens to you! He said, "The world forgets and the world forgives!" He said, "The person it's hardest on is you. You beat yourself up on your apparent failure, but you can learn that failure is feedback. As you get that feedback, you can adapt, you can learn, you can move forward." So being afraid to make a decision in business or anywhere else is actually going to slow you down; it's going to inhibit you from taking any action whatsoever, and then you will never ever know what's going to work or not, because the fear is going to lock you into a victim mentality and you won't move forward.

I have found, and I have said it many times, that when you face your fears, you usually find your wealth, that your wealth is behind the thing you fear. Something that you fear to do is probably something that you *have* to do. My rule of thumb is, if there is something I'm afraid of doing, I should *do it*—it could have been my first public speaking event; it could have been when releasing *Spiritual Marketing* as a book. When I was afraid of doing something, it's because my ego was afraid of being hurt. When I faced my fear and I did it anyway, those events became life changing. When I gave my very first talk, I was quite young. There were six people in the room. I was so nervous I leaned against the wall because I thought I was going to pass out and slide to the floor. I repeatedly faced my fears until, now, I have appeared on *Larry King* and *Donnie Deutsch*; I have appeared onstage before Donald Trump; I have done things that I never thought I would do! One of the highlights for me was to be a keynote speaker for the National Speakers Association—there were 5,000 professional speakers in the audience listening to me, and I received a standing ovation at the end.

Stretch Past Uneasiness

Joe: My point is, I never would have gotten to that place had I not faced my fears in the beginning. I remind people that fear doesn't mean, "Don't take action." Fear is kind of an alert that you're about to do something that you haven't done before. Just be aware. You're about to go into business, or buy a stock, or open a restaurant—who knows what it might be—but because you haven't done it before, you're a little uneasy about it. That uneasiness isn't fear, it's the discomfort that comes from doing something that's a stretch for you.

Again, take a deep breath, look within, and say, "Is this really something that's a life-or-death situation? Should I really be afraid that I'm going to lose my life if I go forward? Or am I uneasy only because I'm stretching my comfort zone?" If it's stretching your comfort zone, face your fear and do it.

Move into a Relaxed Mentality

Theresa Pushkar: While we're talking about business and stretching ourselves, I'm thinking about the world and how we're all feeling very stretched. Everything's rush, rush, rush. Our nervous systems are feeling like they're maxed. What would you say, based on the four stages in the work that you do, this is all about? And how do I deal with the sense of rush and anxiety and hurriedness in my life today?

Joe: Well, the sense of being rushed right now and feeling the stress of the world is actually coming from the first stage—victimhood. "It's the whole world that's bearing down on me and making me feel like I have no control; I can't get anything done. I'm going to go crazy here. There's no time. There's not enough money. There's not enough anything. Not enough energy." Well, that's being a victim. Again, realize that the first stage is okay. You wake up from it and you move into another stage.

When you feel more empowered, for example, you start to imagine, "Well, maybe if I took a few minutes every day to relax. Maybe if I learned how to take three deep breaths as I go about my day. Maybe if I learn to close my eyes, for just a couple of minutes, before I make my next phone call. Maybe as I learn to meditate every day or to work out every day or to do some walking every day." Maybe you need to get a massage once a week or once a month, whatever is possible for you, realize you have more control than you ever thought possible.

So, you start to move into this relaxed mentality that says the world might be driving itself crazy, but you don't have to drive yourself crazy. You can actually take care of yourself, love yourself, pamper yourself, while still getting things done. Try to determine what stage of awareness you are in. If you've awakened to being a victim, that's fine. But you can take control and move into the next stage of awakening and actually feel like you're empowered and start to use some of those techniques to help you feel as though you're getting things done at your own time and pace. And I have to remind you, in Stage Three you surrender.

You Don't Have to Handle It All Yourself

Joe: In Stage Three, you're talking to the Divine and saying, "Look, I can't handle all the stress. I can't handle all the busyness. I can't handle all the activity that's going on in the world." There's a wonderful healing technique from Hawaii called *ho'oponopono*. You don't have to remember the long word. Basically, it's a simple technique in which you take complete responsibility for everything in your life. You forgive everybody in your life. And you love everybody in your life, beginning with yourself. As a clearing and cleansing technique to help you get to a place of being at peace in this moment, you repeat the following phrases: "I'm sorry. Please forgive me. Thank you. I love you."

Beyond the Busyness

Joe: When you're in this moment, it's funny, but all the busyness of the world isn't really busy.

Theresa Pushkar: Thank you. We're talking about the busyness of the moment—I'm thinking about women, mothers—and there seems to be an epidemic of "I can't take care of myself. I've got to take care of everyone else." Now, I have my own issues around that, and then there's mass consciousness and the world issues around that, where we've seen that generations of women before us have been sacrificing themselves for their families. Now I feel like I'm trying to break free, not only of my own issues but those generational issues that exist. Do you have any suggestions or advice for how I might do that?

Joe: Yeah, I do. A couple thoughts come to mind. First of all, you just spoke a belief. There's a belief that keeps getting restated and reactivated in women: that they have to do everything, or they don't have the power, or they have to give in to somebody else. There's this whole mind-set that if you listen closely sounds like a victim mind-set, but the victim mind-set is coming from a belief. So, first of all, do the little belief-clearing exercise I talked about earlier, where I said, "You can question the belief." For example, "Do I really believe that I have to do everything? Do I really believe that I have to do what all women have done before me?" And, as you question it, you uncover the basis for that belief, which almost certainly is a belief that has been handed down to you. You didn't consciously choose this when you were a young girl, it's something that came along a little later. When you realize that you chose this belief, you can let it go and replace it with something more empowering. You can also use the clearing technique, where you say: "I love you. I'm sorry. Please forgive me. Thank you." You're using the Self I-dentity Ho'oponopono technique on that belief and, more important, on any and all beliefs that may be related to it. You don't have to know exactly which beliefs are giving you this feeling, but when you have the feeling, go ahead and hold on to it for a moment and look toward the Divine or toward God, whatever is right for you, and say: "I'm sorry, I don't know where this feeling came from. I don't know where this belief came from. Please forgive me for whatever role I played in creating this unconsciously in my life, and thank you for taking care of it, thank you for releasing it, thank you for clearing and cleansing it." Then end, as I do, with, "I love you," a strong statement of love to the Divine. You are the Divine, saying, "I love you" to the Divine. This in and of itself can clear that belief and all related beliefs, so you start to feel as though you have power: You can do what you need to do when you need to do it.

It's Never about the Other Person

Theresa Pushkar: As you talk beliefs, I'm thinking of the next question and thinking, "Oh, oh, here's a belief. The struggle of the partner. I so believe in the work you do and I've been practicing it. However, my partner, my husband, my wife, doesn't necessarily buy in or isn't on the same path as me. And I struggle with this."

Joe: Notice what you just said, "I struggle with this." This is the ego against outer circumstances one more time. And it means that there's the victim mentality going on. This isn't bad. We all slide between these different stages until we get to the fourth stage and we're actually awakened. So, it's not unusual to fall, in certain areas, into a victim thought pattern. And that's what's going on here. Again, I would say that you want to look at the beliefs that would create that.

You want to use the Self I-dentity Ho'oponopono to clear that. More important, realize that whatever you're looking at, this other person or any other person, is actually a mirror projection of what you're feeling within yourself.

The outer entity is a reflection of your internal state of mind. If there's somebody on the outside, whether it's your partner or your boss, who is feeling like, "You're not making any sense, I'm not on the same page as you," that, in some way, shape, or form is a miscommunication. That person actually represents a part of you that feels that way. That's a biggie. We're talking about the shadow side of your life. We're talking about the part you don't actually want to look at. However, when you own that, you can change that.

In my own case, if somebody says something to me that I think is irritating or that I don't like, I look within myself and say, "Does some part of me believe that?" And, if I'm very honest I realize, "Yeah." There's what we would call a subpersonality that believes that whatever that person said is actually true for me. And that person voiced it, which is irritating me because I didn't want to see it. I didn't want to believe it. I didn't want to own it. So, instead of dealing with that outer person, I deal with that inner self within me.

I may have a dialogue with it. I may ask it, "Why do you believe what you believe? Why are you saying that?" I do it until I get to a place of peace and serenity. And when I do, son of a gun, that outer person who was objecting is no longer objecting. That outer person is now at peace, too. How did the other person change? Because *I* changed on the inside and that person was a reflection of my inside.

If You Work on the Inside, the Outside Changes

Theresa Pushkar: Could that not, then, be an ego trap of my own? If I just keep doing my work and keep telling myself and keep cleaning and clearing this? That, somehow, I'm going to convince my husband to get out of his lack of consciousness, for example?

Joe: Well, actually, that is what you are doing. The more you work on yourself, the more you change the other person, and the world itself. This is why I tell people, if you want world peace, you begin by finding peace within you. I've often said that if you want the planet to be healthy, wealthy, and wise, contribute one healthy, wealthy, and wise person to it. You. You work on yourself and, as you work on yourself, yes, your husband changes or leaves. Or the people around you change or leave. Or the planet changes. Or somehow, you don't become part of what's going on. It all rearranges itself, compared to what's going on within you.

You do have far more control than what you ever imagined. When you work on the inside, it changes the outside.

Group Consciousness Creates Anything and Everything

Theresa Pushkar: While we're talking about the planet, there's a lot going on right now. A lot of fear. A lot of natural disasters. Based on the work you've done and the four stages, what's your call on what's happening to the planet?

Joe: Well, with group consciousness, we're creating anything and everything. For example, people who are in areas that have a flood or a fire or an earthquake or a famine have all cocreated that, but on an unconscious level. These people are not meeting and saying something like, "Let's have a flood here." What's going on is that they have an unconscious desire for that. They don't know it, any more than you or I fully know what's in our unconscious minds.

They've come in and they've attracted each other. We attract, into groups, based on what our mentality is. What our unconscious belief system is. So all of these people have gathered together in these areas, and they do go through a victim mentality mind-set. Part of the purpose is for them to awaken from it and possibly to grow from it, and part of it is for us to awaken from it. You don't have to actually be in the flood physically to have the experience of it. You watch the news. You watch the media. You see it over the Internet. And you realize that in some way, shape or form, you cocreated it.

It's Yours if It's in Your Experience

Joe: This goes back to what Dr. Hew Len had taught me. If something is in your experience, if you are complaining about something, whatever the problem is, do you notice you're there? That you are always there? You're the common element. When you hear about the earthquake or the fire or the flood or the breakdown or the terrorists, whatever it happens to be, and you note that you don't like that, realize that you helped create it. Because it's in your reality. This is why constant cleaning is so important.

This is why the Self I-dentity Ho'oponopono is so important. If you really want to stop all of that from happening and change the world and change these disasters from taking place, you want to say, "I'm sorry. I don't know what in my unconscious mind contributed to this taking place, any more than those people did. Please forgive me for whatever I said, whatever I did, whatever energy I have given out to participate in this. Thank you for taking care of this. For healing it. And I love you. I love you. I love you." This is on all of us to do.

Again, people have been victims. We've all played that role, but we were not doing it consciously. We've been doing it unconsciously. That's why awakening is crucial. That's the whole point.

Theresa Pushkar: I sense that some people could become outraged by your last suggestion: "How dare you say that I created this flood? How dare you?" There seems to be a sense of immediate wanting to fight back and make you the enemy. And there has to be some step within that can take them to a place of understanding—I don't know whether it's more compassion for themselves or for you.

"Whose Energy Is It?"

Theresa Pushkar: Is there some bridge between them being able to take responsibility, to do the ho'oponopono, and immediately wanting to attack you and say, "How dare you say that I created this?"

Joe: Yeah, that's a very good question and a very raw and honest question. People who immediately respond with anger don't like to hear that; they are upset with me for being the one who said that. Guess which stage they're coming from? Stage One, Victimhood. How do I get them to cross over to the next stage? Well, I have to do it. This is coming from my surrendered mindset. This is coming from the stage of surrendering to the Divine and realizing that everything in my personal, Joe Vitale, experience, is being caused by what Joe Vitale is doing within himself.

If somebody is in my face saying, "You are outrageous for making such a wild claim," I have to take a deep breath and realize that some part of me agrees with that person. When I do, I look within myself and say, "I have no idea which part that is. I have no idea why it's there." And I clean on it. I clear it. I remove it. As I do, those people don't show up in my experience. They might exist someplace on the planet, and they might still have that feeling, but they don't show up in my experience. Why not? Because I cleared it out.

I advise people to look at how it feels to be angry. How does it feel to be a victim? How does it feel to send all of your rage and your energy outward? A friend of mine once pointed out somebody who was very upset all the time about politics and things that were going on in the political system. That person was enraged by it. But that person was not a politician. That person was not in the government body. That person wasn't taking any action. So my friend asked that person, "Who's energy system are you burning up when you feel that rage?"

Well, obviously, the person who was feeling the rage was destroying his own body, his own mind, his own lifestyle, his own happiness by feeling rage. It's of no use. I advise you to consider that maybe you're being a victim. Maybe you'd like to go into the second stage of awakening and be more empowered. And I look within myself and say, "What part of me has contributed to what I'm seeing?" Then I clean on it.

There's Nothing to Be Afraid Of

Theresa Pushkar: Thank you. Your responses to many of the questions I've asked have been about falling into victimhood consciousness. I see a universe, a world, that has created a certain mind-set within us. And it appears that this mind-set is very different, perhaps, than that which the universe really holds. Can you share your insights on some of the misguided paths that we follow, compared to the truth of the universe?

Joe: Well, the truth of the universe is, there's nothing to be afraid of. That's one of the reoccurring themes in almost all of these spiritual teachings: "Do not be afraid. Fear not." And almost everybody who comes from a victim mentality or an ego mentality is afraid. They're afraid of everything. They're afraid of the next thing they're going to say, or what somebody's going to say to them, or the next turn in the road, or the next job interview. Whatever it happens to be, they're afraid.

The universe basically says, "You are taken care of. There is nothing to be afraid of. We love you." At the essence, at the core, the Divine, the universe itself, is all love. That's the main discrepancy right there: In the ego mentality, individuals think that they need to protect themselves. And the Divine, the universe, is trying to say, "Drop the control. Drop the protection. Even drop your mind." When you do, you're at the state of awakening, where you are one with the Divine, if not actually the Divine itself.

Is There a God?

Theresa Pushkar: There is a deluge of books right now, best sellers, offering the premise that God doesn't exist, that "God is a fallacy to make us all feel secure and comfortable." What's your response to this?

Joe: Well, there's some truth to it, because there are a lot of beliefs about God and the Divine that are actually created by humans. I've always loved this quote by Mark Twain: "The Bible said something to the effect of 'God was made in man's image.'" And he paused and said, "I wonder who said that?" Well, of course, it was a human! It's the ego extension trying to project outward. "What is God like? What is the Divine like?" Well, probably a lot like us. That's the limit of our understanding. When the scientific community looks at God as a Supreme Being with a long, gray beard and some sort of image or visual that they're trying to track through the universe, and they can't find such an entity, it doesn't mean there isn't any divinity there. It doesn't mean that there isn't this Supreme Being behind everything, including inside you. Including inside those scientists. It means they're barking up the wrong tree. It means they're looking in the wrong area, and they're looking for something they will never find, because they have the wrong description for what they're looking for.

Could This Be the Greatest Thing That Ever Happened?

Theresa Pushkar: I've heard two different trains of thoughts on accidents and illnesses. One of them is, "I take full responsibility." You run to the book and find out which core emotion is related to that particular dysfunctional organ in the body, saying, "Okay, there's some kind of mental, emotional block I have that is creating this." Other people get very upset and say, "How dare you say I created this? Accidents happen. Injuries, cancer, disease happens. It has nothing to do with my consciousness." What's your take on that?

Joe: Well, there are at least two ways to look at this. One is, if you come from Stage One, Victimhood, you will be outraged by it because you'll think, "Accidents do happen" and "I'm just a victim of one of those accidents." But if you come from Stage Two, Empowerment, you'll look a little deeper and think, "Maybe I did in some way, shape, or form, attract this, create this, or welcome this."

There are many stories of people who have had cancer, or were in a bad car accident, or were overtaken by some sort of disaster who, although traumatized for a while, came out and said that it was the greatest thing that ever happened to them. They looked back and thought, "Wow, I guess I attracted this so that I would become a musician, or go a different route with my business, or meet such-and-such a person whom I may never otherwise have met." They found a positive reason for it. And then they congratulated themselves for setting this up to happen.

This seems preposterous until you start reading stories like Lance Armstrong's, who has said that cancer was one of the greatest things that ever happened to him and the reason he's a world-class athlete. He's a legend in modern times. He'll go down in history. Yet he was motivated by something that other people might say was absolutely horrible, that would have stopped them in their tracks as long as they were victims and remained victims.

You can continue to be a victim and think, "The accident happened, and I was a victim of it." Or you can say, "The accident happened, and I actually participated in the creation of it and I participated in turning it into something good. And I grew from it." As with most things in life, you have a choice about how you perceive events. You have a choice about how you perceive so-called accidents.

Theresa Pushkar: So, the externals are what they are. It's our perceptions that make a difference.

Joe: The externals are absolutely what they are, but to take a more divine perspective, you did attract them. I'm not dismissing the fact that you attracted these things. I'm suggesting that you have a choice about how you look at them. If you look at them as a victim, you will just push them aside; you'll put some distance between them and you. And you won't actually learn from them, except, perhaps, to say, "Maybe I won't drink when I drive tonight."

However, you can learn more than that, and you can see the deeper connection that, on an unconscious level, you've created a little scene, a little act, where an accident took place. But you created that scene, that act, that tragedy to learn something. And when you learn it, you grow.

Even at the Top, You Never Stop Growing

Theresa Pushkar: As you discuss the four stages, I look forward and I pray that at some point I will be graced to be experiencing Stage Four. Is there a point, then, for example, Stage Four, where you don't need any more books? You don't need any more audio? You don't need any external guidance? That literally all the answers come from within you?

Joe: That's an interesting question. I'm not in Stage Four. I'm more of a journalist who is reporting on it. I know of it. I've had various satori experiences that have given me glimpses into it. But I'm just like you. I'm still growing. I'm still evolving. I'm still becoming more and more aware. As I understand it, you will still want to read, watch TV, eat spaghetti, go dancing, have wonderful experiences. You're just doing it with a different level of awareness.

You're still growing. You're still learning. It doesn't mean that you're suddenly the old, wise computer that can answer every question about life or death. It means that you're still growing. You're still learning. You're still struggling in some respects, in some areas, but you're doing it with this deep level of trust. You're doing it with this deep understanding that you're playing a role in a cosmic drama, in a cosmic play. And you have fun with it, at that point. Then you can laugh at virtually everything, because you know that, on some level, you're detached from it. On some level, you've created it, because you're part of the Divine.

And, on some level, you know you're absolutely fine, because, when it's all over, you're just merging right back with the Divine. So, you don't stop learning. You don't just unplug your life. You're actually more plugged into life at that stage, as I understand it.

Authenticity Is a Key

Theresa Pushkar: I was just reminded, with your last response, of your great candor. I find it very refreshing and very humbling on your part to share, "This is my journey. I'm on it with you." You say it with great confidence, with a great sense of acceptance. I'm thinking of those of us who are on the journey, Stage One, Stage Two, where it's really tough to look at ourselves and to own and be responsible, as part of ourselves, that aren't where we'd like to be. How do you find the confidence to be able to declare it with a lot of love and compassion for the self?

Joe: Wow. Well, first of all, thank you for the compliment. Second, I don't know any other way to be. I think that authenticity is part of the key of going through all of these stages. I think being totally honest with yourself is a way of going forward in awakening. That, if you lie to yourself at any stage, you won't grow, because you are trying to deceive yourself. When I openly say that I was homeless or that I'm not awakened or enlightened, I'm actually stating it for myself and for the universe.

I think at some point in my life I realized that when I lied to anybody, I was lying to the universe, I was lying to the Divine. And I was teaching it not to trust me. I was teaching it, and myself, not to trust myself. If I lied to you about wherever I was in my position, in the world, in my life, in my struggles, if I lied to you, it made it better than it really was. And then I prayed to the universe, to God, to the Divine and said, "Please bring me such and such" or "Please help me with such and such."

The Divine would say, "I don't know if you really want that or not. Because you've already stated that you're not to be trusted." I've learned that total authenticity, right down to where it hurts, means that you tell the truth. It's ruthless honesty. Some people have come to me and said, "I don't know what I want. I don't know what I want to ask for. I don't know what I want to do with my life or be or act on." And I say, "You're actually lying. You're lying to yourself and you're lying to me."

If you were to be ruthlessly honest with yourself—and I purposely say the word *ruthlessly* so you don't dodge around the word *honest*—you know in your heart what you've always longed to do. You've been afraid to speak it, because as soon as you speak it you have to take responsibility for not doing it. And that gets a little scary for a lot of people who are in the victim mentality.

So, for me, it begins with total authenticity. Be honest about who you are, what you're doing, what you're trying to achieve, what you're trying to attract, what you would like to experience in your life, where you are with your life. I think the universe respects that. I think other people respect that, and I think it helps you fall into line with the whole awareness process, the evolutionary process. Truth is king. Being ruthlessly honest is a spiritual quest.

Theresa Pushkar: That was very powerful. I've got a tricky one now for you.

Denial Gets You Nowhere, Except Where You Don't Want to Be

Joe: Okay.

Theresa Pushkar: Denial. For example, take someone who is passive-aggressive. I recently heard from a psychologist that if you're passive-aggressive you don't know that you are. So, how do those who don't know they are passive-aggressive or don't know they are in denial, because they have such a thick skin of protection around them, ever begin to awaken?

Joe: That's a curious question. Because it's people who are in the victimhood stage who are about to be empowered. I'm saying that because if they are denying who they are, what they want, their experiences, their problems, all of that, then they are in the victimhood stage. They're saying that they don't have to take control, that they don't have to take responsibility. They are in some way, shape, or form dismissing all of it. Unfortunately, if you remember when you asked about those accidents that happened, accidents may happen to these kinds of people. Something will jar them awake.

I'm almost reluctant to say it, because I don't want to feel as though I'm planting that as a suggestion, but I've found more often than not, people who are not facing the shadow side of themselves—who are falling into denial, who are not admitting what they really want—at some point hit what others call "the bottom." I really think that happened to me when I was homeless for so long. People say, "What woke you up to realize that you were modeling your life after destructive characters like Jack London and Ernest Hemingway? They were wonderful authors, but they weren't so great at their lifestyle." Yet I was modeling my life after them and "going down the tubes," so to speak.

I think what woke me up is that I hit bottom. I looked around and realized, "I'm sleeping in a toilet stall. I'm sleeping on a church pew. I am not happy. I am not succeeding. I am not getting anywhere." I might have been telling everybody, coming from my denial mind-set, "I'm an author. I'm going to get published. I am going to achieve great things." But there I was, homeless. Homeless and in poverty. I think that an awakening comes because your unconscious mind says, "As long as you're going to be asleep, we're going to do something to wake you up." That's when you start to go into Stage Two.

I'd rather have you go into Stage Two because of *The Awakening Course*. Because of a movie like *The Secret* or books by my friends John Assaraf, Lisa Nichols, Jack Canfield, or Bob Proctor—any of these wonderful souls—so that you don't have a painful awakening, but rather an easy one.

Theresa Pushkar: The good news is that those reading are already there. They study the program with the sense of, "Oh that's Joe, my brother. Oh, there's so and so, my sister. Oh, there's my boss." And if they don't actually absorb the words and the teachings that you have and look at themselves and say, "Oh, there I am," then perhaps they can reread the program and keep triggering back to the self until they understand that they are responsible for their lives.

Joe: I would agree. It's a good to remember that if you have this book in your hands, if you're reading this right now, it means that you've passed the victimhood stage. You're actually empowering yourself. Because studying *The Awakening Course* is an empowering experience. You had to actually raise your hand and say, "I want to be awake. I want to grow. I want to go to the next level." Congratulations. That has to be a good feeling. In that sense, you've left victimhood, and you are empowered and becoming more empowered.

Balance Is the Key to Breaking Addiction

Theresa Pushkar: I guess another area, as far as not seeing or denial, is that in our society we have a lot of addictions that are generally accepted. Addictions to television. Sexual addiction. Addiction to computers. Ways that people can avoid living or avoid their problems and immerse themselves in these things. Addiction to eating or exercise. Things that are often perceived as a good thing can be overdone.

Joe: Absolutely. I also want to point out that there's a book by William Glassner called *Positive Addiction*. There *is* such a thing as positive addiction. Running, working out, for example, those are considered positive addictions. If you're doing them to the extent that you don't show up at work or you're not paying any attention to your family, it's probably a negative addiction. You're probably taking it a little too far in one direction.

Balance is the key. I really feel that addiction is another form of being a victim. That you're trying to overcompensate in some painful area. There's something you don't want to face. There's something you don't want to do and you've found a way to escape. An addiction could be TV. It could be eating. It could be exercise. It could be smoking. It could be any number of things that you know are harmful to you.

The Greatest Leaps: Getting Help When You Need It

Joe: I am a great believer in getting help when you need it. I've started a Miracles Coaching program that I think you know about. And in the Miracles Coaching program, people get encouragement, they get support, they get information, they get inspiration.

I have found that I have made the greatest leaps in my life by having a personal coach. Coaching, of course, is very popular in the athletic area. Baseball players, football players, they all have coaches. And now people in business have coaches. People in relationships have coaches. People with wine collections have coaches. There are all kinds of coaches for all kinds of people. If people feel they are addicted to something and they're not able to break it off by themselves, I say raise your hand and get help. There is nothing wrong with that.

Throughout my career, whenever I have come across a bump in the road and I couldn't get myself out, one of my secrets to success is that I know a lot of different clearing techniques. I know a lot of different ways to make myself feel better. But if I'm still feeling stuck and still feeling like I'm addicted to this problem or this person or this substance, whatever it happens to be, or a nagging problem just won't go away, I know to call for help. I have my own Miracles Coaches. I have my own Miracles Coaches whom I will call.

So, I encourage people to ask for help. Don't try to be a Lone Ranger. I tried to do that for a long time, and you cannot succeed all by yourself. Not easily, anyway.

Theresa Pushkar: The wonder of coaching, I have found, is that you have somebody to answer to and to be accountable to. Many of us consider ourselves highly disciplined. Yet you can up the ante when you have a Coach who is compassionate, who hears, but who calls you on your stuff and asks you, "What are you going to bring me next week? What have you got?"

Accountability Is a Big Thing

Joe: Yes. I think that's very important. Accountability is a big thing. You are more likely to act if you know that next Monday you're going to be talking to your Coach and the Coach is going to ask you, "Did you work out three times a week? Did you work on your novel? Did you open your business or write a business plan?" You're more likely to do it than if you didn't have a Coach. Some people are disciplined enough to get it done, but I find that when you have a Coach, you actually do more. You're more accelerated in your progress, and you are happier about it, because you have somebody to share it with—somebody who's urging you on, who's rooting you on, who's a cheerleader in your corner. Having a Coach is a big secret to success.

Theresa Pushkar: How often do you have a captive listener who's literally totally focusing on you and totally loving you and encouraging you?

Joe: Yes. That's priceless.

The Difference between Knowing and Experiencing

Theresa Pushkar: Yes. I'm also wondering about experiencing versus knowing. I'm sure many of the readers may have listened to several programs and read several books. They know this material. They haven't experienced it yet. And it's a big difference. I struggle with that myself.

Joe: Yes, knowing and experiencing are two different things. When I talked about meditation earlier, for example, you may have shook your head and said, "Oh, I've meditated before." But you may have a very different experience when I talked about meditation in the marketplace, where you walk through your day and you're actually meditating as you're working, you're meditating as you're breathing. You're just conscious of what's going on.

It's the difference between reading a recipe for a particular dessert and actually eating the dessert. Eating the recipe itself is not very fulfilling. But eating the dessert might be actually very yummy for you. I have an intellectual understanding of the fourth stage of awakening, but I don't have it as an experiential experience. I actually have moments of it, and I relish those moments and welcome more of them, but I know that I have to keep working.

I still meditate every day. I still do the gratitude moments every day. I still do the Self I-dentity Ho'oponopono every day and, in fact, almost every minute. Because I know there's so much work to be done, and the more I do, the more I prep myself for the awakening, the enlightenment, the satori, for whatever is next. Knowing, on an intellectual level, isn't enough. It prepares you for what's to come, but it's only one step in that direction. It's not the final step.

It's Not Work

Theresa Pushkar: When you talk about work, I know that as you say *work,* you mean something brings great joy.

Joe: Yes.

Theresa Pushkar: Can you share your insights about that?

Joe: Well, that's a great question. Because when I say *work,* I don't mean work the way most people mean it. Most people go to a nine-to-five job, then complain about it, and they consider that to be work. But I am a very prolific and productive individual. I've written maybe 50 books. I've produced a couple of different audio programs, many different DVDs, a home study course, a Miracles Coaching program, an Executive Mentoring program. I do all kind of seminars. I do speaking engagements. I'm actively working on a blog. I'm involved in social media sites. I'm involved in Twitter and Facebook and MySpace. The list goes on.

People wonder, "How do you do so much work?" Well, it's not work, it's fun! I'm smiling to think about it, because I really look forward to writing. I really look forward to participating. I really look forward to moments like this when I get to share what I've discovered. I'm happy for other people who are eager to learn from it and to grow from it. I just can't wait to keep doing it. So it's not work. It's activity, but it's activity that is so exhilarating and so joyful that I can't stop doing it.

I might have used the word *work,* and occasionally still use it, but it's because I'm getting things done. It's just a phrase and a definition. For me, it doesn't have the emotional baggage or the negative connotation that it might for people who don't like their work. I *like* my work. It's my play.

Share the Fun

Theresa Pushkar: Well, sitting across from you, I hear the energy that you exude. Clearly, it energizes you; it's your passion; you're in the zone, and therefore *effort* sounds like a thing of the past for you.

Joe: You're absolutely right. For the most part, effort is something in my past. I do my best to do only the things that are fun for me to do. If something needs to be done that I don't think is fun—for example, my taxes—I give it an accountant who thinks it's fun! In this, way I circulate wealth and keep everybody happy. This is really how the world works. We all play different parts. What's fun for me may not be fun for you. What's fun for the accountant may not be fun for me or you. We find people who enjoy the tasks that need to be done, and we employ them; they in turn employ us to do what we do. In that way we follow our calling and the world works!

When You're Done, You're Done

Theresa Pushkar: That brings about another question. I recently heard from a spiritual teacher that when you're repulsed by something, you're done with it. It's over. This is contrary to another teaching I've heard that if you're repulsed by something, there's something in there for you, something you don't want to look at within yourself. Yet I heard that when you're repulsed by something, when you're deeply repulsed, you're done. And that made me feel a sense of, "Oh, that felt right and that felt good." But there's a real conflict there. What are your views on this?

Joe: Well, I don't understand the first one at all. "When you're repulsed by something, you're done" doesn't make any sense to me. Because in my world, the way I understand how the world works, when you're repulsed by something, it's a reflection that you have the very thing that's upsetting you *within* you. You may have it as a judgment. You may have it as a quality. But it's pushing a button within you. I think it's good news to find something that's upsetting to you or repulsing to you, because then you get to clear it. When you clear it and cleanse it within yourself by loving it, finding out what the belief is behind it, at that point, you're free from it.

You may find that after this process of clearing and cleansing, the same thing that repulsed you one day will mean nothing to you the next time you see it. It will be like reading a story in a book. It will have no energy, no negativity to it; you will be clear of it. But to be repulsed, to be "done with it," I don't know what that means.

Unconditional Love Is the Goal

Theresa Pushkar: So, that's the point of unconditional love, where literally you've cleared everything so nothing triggers you. Nothing creates anger or frustration. There's compassion in your response.

Joe: I love that. Unconditional love is, I think, our goal—unconditional love in every aspect of your life, in everything around you. If you can look at something, no matter what it is, and say that it's love, it came from God, it came from the Divine, and you have no judgment on it, you're at an awakened place. You must be awakened, at that point, as far as I'm concerned. If you can see a cockroach and say, "I love it," if you can see something that repulsed you in the past and say, "I can see why I love that. I can see what its value is and the positivity in it, how it's serving everything," then you are awakened.

When you get to the point where you're unconditionally accepting of everything, of all in your life, then you are at a point of enlightenment, or of something next door to it.

Forgive Everybody for Everything—Including Yourself

Theresa Pushkar: That brings up the subject of forgiveness. You know, forgiveness, from what I've heard, doesn't sell in the self-help world. We have such a reluctance to forgive. Knowing that I'm depleting my own energy by not forgiving and yet still struggling to forgive.

Joe: Wow. I'm so glad you brought that up. Forgiveness is probably one of the most powerful clearing and cleansing techniques there is. I did not talk about it earlier in this interview. So, thank you for bringing it up. We need to address that. My rule of thumb is, if you have a block anywhere in your life, it's probably because you have not forgiven yourself or somebody involved who is related to that block. Very often, we have done things in the past that we regret. We said something. We did something. You know, when we're young we all make mistakes.

When we're growing up, we still do. Most of us don't forgive ourselves. We hold onto that. We beat ourselves up. Very often, we beat ourselves up unconsciously. Forgiving yourself, forgiving others is the most powerful thing you can do to free your energy.

When you haven't forgiven yourself or somebody else in your life, you're still carrying around the past. If you are not in this moment, you're actually in the past or in the future.

And if you haven't forgiven somebody, including yourself, you're still in the past. You're carrying around the charge or the energy, the mind-set, the beliefs, the grudge, the regret, whatever it happens to be. You *must* forgive. I don't care if it's not big in the self-help market. I don't care what they think about that. Because I know that the single most dramatically influential thing you can do is to actually take an inventory of those whom you need to forgive. It might even be something worth writing about.

Make a "Forgiveness" List

Joe: Find a place to sit down and write about it on a sheet of paper or in your journal. List all the things that happened, then forgive everybody involved. In fact, what comes to mind as I'm talking and ad-libbing in front of you is, when I discussed being a victim earlier in this book, I asked readers to make a list of all the times when they felt like victims. It would be wonderful to go through that list now and forgive everybody involved.

That might be a tall order, but you can just kind of eat away at it and do it a little bit every day. You're saying to people who were involved, "I'm sorry. I forgive you. I forgive myself. I forgive everybody involved." You might even do the Self I-dentity Ho'oponopono: Feel what you're feeling and ask the Divine to help you forgive. "Please forgive me. I'm sorry. Thank you. I love you."

I think this is the bonus tip from the Divine here, that if you actually want to take care of all the blocks in your path so you are free to move forward without any baggage, go back and forgive yourself and everybody involved. That is probably, as I take a deep breath and think about this, an astonishingly wonderful and transformative thing to do. Forgive yourself and all others.

Radical Forgiveness

Joe: Radical forgiveness means you realize that nothing bad ever even happened. That's radical forgiveness—when you get to the mind-set, with unconditional love, of realizing that nothing bad happened.

I see that it was actually good, that I actually grew from it. Or they grew from it. Or we transformed because of it. When you get to the point where you realize that nothing bad happened, you are free. You are free.

Ask the Divine to Help You Forgive

Theresa Pushkar: That's a wonderful insight. At one point when you were speaking, I was thinking, "I'm so struggling to forgive this person" and "I'm so beating myself up for not being able to forgive, knowing the energy I'm losing if I'm not willing to let this go." If I just keep saying, to the Divine and to myself, "I'm sorry, please forgive me," that, in and of itself is clearing and cleansing.

Joe: What you're doing is asking for help. And that's a very wise thing to do. If you do feel like you're stuck and you can't ask for forgiveness for yourself or somebody else, for whatever reason, you can turn to the Divine and in a prayerful way say, "This is bigger than what I can handle. Please help me with it. Please forgive me. I'm sorry. Thank you. I love you." Actually do the process on the very feeling of not being able to forgive. Let the Divine help you.

What I've learned is that the Divine will answer if you ask.

Theresa Pushkar: We just don't ask enough, do we?

Joe: No, we don't.

Theresa Pushkar: Well, Joe, thank you so much. There are many, many more questions. Yet there will also be many, many more programs, I'm sure.

Joe: Well, let me leave you with a thought. Dr. Hew Len, with whom I coauthored the book *Zero Limits*, says, "Questions are simply from the mind." And if you actually let them come and let them go, you are one step closer to the Divine.

Chapter 8

Bonus Chapter
What Do You Want?

I'm discovering that if you want to have deep and personal and permanent change in yourself and in the planet, you need to consider that you're more responsible for everything in your life, including the lives of everybody else, than you ever fathomed.

—Joe Vitale

Can you imagine what your life would be like if you received everything you ever wished for? New cars, more money, a dream home, your soul mate, a yacht, the cure for a disease, or anything else you wanted. How would you like to attract a miracle today?

What do you want? A new car?
What do you want? A new house?
What do you want? Health and vitality?
What do you want? Money to build and invest?
What do you want? Progressive legislation?
What do you want? A community garden?
What do you want? Time to give back?
What do you want? Love?
What do you want? Wealth?
What else? World peace?

Miracles Can Happen in an Instant

How many of you want a miracle? Do you want one or not? How many of you want a miracle today, in the next 40 minutes? I don't believe you. How many of you want a miracle today, in the next 40 minutes? What?

Are you getting everything you want? I have some yeses, some *not* yeses, and some nos. Have you gotten everything that you want? Everything? Are you done? You're not done. That's right, you wouldn't be here if you were done. There's more that you want. My question to you is, if you want more and you don't have it right now, why not? Some of you cry. What is this?

I want to talk about *The Missing Secret*. I hope you've seen *The Secret*. I happened to walk in here today with somebody as I was heading to my booth, and, when I told her that I had a booth, she said, "What do you do?" I said, "I'm an author, and I was in a movie called *The Secret*." She said, "What's that?" Isn't it amazing? It's amazing because the movie's been out for two years, yet there are people who have never heard of it, but for those of you who have heard of it and have practiced it, how many of you think it won't work? Okay, how many want to say yes but are afraid to raise your hands? Yes, there are some hands going up.

The Universe Rearranges Itself around You

The Law of Attraction is the idea that what you think and what you feel is pulling in your life experiences—the people, the events, everything is coming into you because of your internal vibration. *The Secret* only introduces the idea of the Law of Attraction. It doesn't explain it to the fullest extent, and that's what I want to talk about now.

The missing secret is the idea that when you want something, first you have to define it—you can say, for example, that you want a house, a car. We went through this whole montage up here and kept asking you, "What do you want, what do you want, what do you want, what do you want, what do you want?" Asking you repeatedly is designed to help you answer that question with clarity and purpose, but when you answer it, when you come up with something, what happens next? What happens next? Some of you don't even take action. Some of you are waiting around for something to happen.

One of the criticisms of *The Secret* is that it looks as though you just sit in a chair, imagine the car you want, then go downstairs and find it in the driveway. The movie gives some people that feeling, but that's not the reality of how this works. I'm in the movie; I'm the guy who says, "I'm going to get in your face"; and I'm the guy who says, "The universe likes speed, money likes speed. Action is what makes thing happen." You have a part in the cocreation of miracles, and your part is to take action on inspired ideas.

Say that you've chosen what you want, you say you're taking action on what you want, and yet it's still not happening. You say it's not coming into your experience: You're not getting the job; you're not getting more sales; you're not finding the relationship; you're not healing the problem that you have with health. Whatever it happens to be, it's not happening. What's happening with that? Does that mean the Law of Attraction isn't working?

The Universe Is Always Listening and Responds to You Every Time—No Exceptions

What it means is that the Law of Attraction is working very, very well. It's working on an unconscious level. Your most powerful operating system is not your conscious mind; it is your unconscious mind. Your conscious mind sees through a tiny little window into the universe. It has no clue what's going on, and we identify ourselves with our conscious mind. We think we have control. We don't.

Our unconscious mind is the most powerful operating system, and the unconscious beliefs there are causing you to attract everything you have in your life, and when I say, "everything," there's no escape clause. I mean *everything,* and I'll explain that a little later, because I'm talking about 100 percent responsibility to a degree that makes you at first uncomfortable.

What's going on in the unconscious mind? Say you want money, for example, and you're using affirmations such as, "I want money, I deserve money, I love money, money is my friend," all of those wonderful things that we've learned to do from great books such as *Money Is My Friend* and books that I've written such as *The Attractor Factor.*

You Are Not to Blame—You Are Simply Responsible

You do all of that and visualize having the money. You visualize that things are coming to you exactly the way you want them, but they still don't happen. You have within you counterintentions. It's perfectly fine and dandy to have an intention that says, "I am going to work out three days a week," or "I am going to attract this romance," or "I am going to increase my job sales during this particular week." Whatever it happens to be, it's perfectly fine to have that intention.

However, if you have counterintentions in your unconscious mind that veto your intention, you won't see results, or if you do get results, you will push them away. You will sabotage yourself and find a way to kill your intention, because you don't feel you deserve it. You won't feel you deserve it because of the counterintentions.

I talk about money quite a bit, because 30-odd years ago, I was homeless. Some of you knew that; some heard it on the video that just played. For many years I could not talk about it, because it was a very disturbing time for me and very sad for me to think about. I lived in Dallas at that time, and I found it very difficult to go back to Dallas for a couple of decades. Because there was a dark form and a dark cloud around me and my relationship with Dallas, whenever I would return to Dallas, bad things always happened.

I remember driving into Dallas once, and as soon as I crossed the Dallas County line, the border, the city line, I was pulled over by a cop. How the hell did that happen? I magnetically attracted him, though I did not know it at the time, because I had all this unconscious garbage about Dallas and homelessness that I had not resolved at that point.

We Live in a Belief-Driven Universe: Change Your Beliefs and You Change Your Life

A lot of us have unfinished issues within us that need to be completed; we have beliefs within us, counterintentions, that need to be released.

Some of you may say, "I want more money," and you don't get more money. It's because your counterbeliefs say things like, "Money is the root of all evil." "Money corrupts." "You have to work hard for your money." "Rich people are evil." These are all good reasons why you are conflicted about what you want. These are the popular mass-consciousness beliefs that produce counterintentions.

So, even though you're saying within yourself, "I want more money, I want more money," and you're striving to have more money and watching *The Secret* and reading about the Law of Attraction, you're not succeeding because *unconsciously you're saying*, "Money is bad; money is evil; greedy people are bad; rich people are bad; the corporations are all out to get us. Money's going to take me, and I'll become different." All of this is within you, and that's the more powerful operating system.

You're trying to bring in money with this little weak attempt, but unconsciously you're pushing it away, and then you say, "It's because of the economy; it's because of the president; it's because of somebody else."

Stage One of Awakening Begins with a Victim Mind-Set

I believe life is a process of awakening. Life is a process of awakening. When we are born, we are born with the consciousness of being a victim. There are exceptions to this, but in general sweeping terms, at birth we're dependent on our parents as our first programmers, then our school system, then our religion, then our government—and none of them are programming us to be empowered.

Again, there are exceptions, but for most of us, myself included, we are born feeling, "I am a victim of circumstances; I am a victim of other people." That's how the vast majority of people lead their lives today, as victims. That's Stage One in the process of awakening.

As you go through this process, you end up at some point seeing a beautiful movie like *The Secret*. There's another movie called *The Opus,* which you might see. There's another movie coming called *Try It on Everything,* which is wonderful. You might read a book like *The Attractor Factor*, or some of Jack Canfield's work or Bob Proctor's, or any of the other people who were in *The Secret* or *The Opus*. At that point, you awaken and you realize, "I don't have to be a victim. I have more power than ever before." You start to take some control. You start to dabble.

Some people will say, "Suddenly I can manifest parking places." How many of you can do that now? It was very easy to park here this weekend because we've all become good at this, right? We've all become good at conjuring parking places, but why we can't manifest bigger things? Those counterintentions are there.

Stage Two: From Victimhood to Empowerment

At some point, you go through Stage Two, and you start to realize that you are awakening, that you have more power than ever before, and you create a more detailed vision. You start stating intentions; you start acting on those intentions; and you start to see enough results that you think, "This is magic, and I believe in magic. I believe in miracles. I believe this is the time of wonder, right now."

Stage Three: From Empowerment to Surrender

Then along comes another book, another movie, another event that precipitates Stage Three. I wrote a book called *Zero Limits*. How many of you have read that? Oh, quite a few of you have read that. *Zero Limits* is probably the most important book that I've written so far. It's a very personal, very intimate, very life-changing book for me and for those who read it. A lot of people read *Zero Limits* or listen to my latest audio program, *The Missing Secret,* because when I tell a certain story in there, they realize Stage Three is about surrender. Stage Three is about becoming a servant to what I call the Divine.

This is where I am, and this is where I'd like you to be today. I began this by saying, "How many of you would like to have a miracle?" and I got a fairly enthusiastic response. How many of you would still like to have a miracle? Okay, you're still with me.

As We Evolve, New Doors Open

In the book *Zero Limits* and in the audio program *The Missing Secret,* I talk about a story, a true story, that I didn't believe when I first heard it. You may not believe it at first, either, but when I first heard this it blew my mind.

The story is about a therapist who worked for a hospital—a hospital for mentally ill criminals in Hawaii, and these mentally ill criminals were dangerous. They were sedated, or they were shackled every day. Hospital employees were quitting. Psychologists would sign on and then leave after 30 days. They couldn't stand it. You'd have to walk down the hall with your back against the wall because you were afraid of being attacked. That's how bad it was. Turnover was dramatic: Nurses would quit, doctors would quit, social workers would quit. This was a hellish place.

100 Percent Responsibility Changes Everything

One therapist who signed on knew a Hawaiian healing technique, and he said, "I will go to the hospital, but I will not work one-on-one with the patients. I will review their files and do my own healing work on them," from the privacy and safety of his own office. He helped heal every one of those mentally ill criminals with this method, and he did it by surrendering to the Divine and by taking 100 percent responsibility for everything that was happening.

This ties in to where I want to take you. I say, "Life is a process of awakening." I say, "This third stage is about surrender." I'm promising you a miracle today. I'm leading up to it for you right now.

I didn't believe that story about the therapist, but I went searching, because I thought, if it's true, I have to know, I have to find him, I have to research him, I have to tell this to the world. I did find him. I studied with him. I've done workshops with him. He and I have done workshops together. His name is Dr. Ihaleakala Hew Len. I just call him Dr. Hew Len. He practices a healing method called *ho'oponopono*. More precisely, it's called Self I-dentity Ho'oponopono. I just call it the Dr. Hew Len method to simplify the name.

You Create Your Own Reality

It's a method for cleaning your unconscious mind by taking 100 percent responsibility and ridding yourself of those counterintentions and beliefs that you're not even aware of. Stick with me on this. He said that we've all heard the phrase "You create your own reality." How many of you have heard that? You create your own reality, yes.

This kind of audience is a more awakened audience. You have heard that phrase; you know that phrase. You probably have a bumper sticker to that effect on your car. You know this, but Dr. Hew Len took it to a level that I never imagined before. It really stretched my mind to a quantum level that was just incredible. He basically said that if you create your own reality, then anybody who shows up in your reality, including a mentally ill criminal, has been created by you, too.

All right, oh my God, even now when I think about this, it is mind-blowing, because this is 100 percent your responsibility; in fact, some people have said it's more than 100 percent your responsibility, maybe 200 percent, because you are responsible for everything going on in your life, and therefore you are responsible for everything going on in everybody else's life who shows up in your life. It seems overwhelming.

You Are Connected to a Power That Is Bigger than You

Dr. Hew Len would look at the patients' charts. Remember, these were mentally ill criminals, violent criminals. They were murderers in many cases. People were afraid of them. Dr. Hew Len would look at the cases, and he would feel what he would feel. It might be rage, frustration, despair, or disappointment. I don't know what he would feel. Whatever he felt, he addressed the Divine. That might mean God to you; that might mean life to you; that might be the globe to you; you might have Gaya. Whatever word you choose, it's the power that is bigger than you, your higher power. Your ego is not in control. This power is bigger than who you think you are, and you're connected to it, and you are of it.

Dr. Hew Len would take his feelings to the Divine and petition with four phrases: "I'm sorry, please forgive me, thank you, and

I love you." "I'm sorry, please forgive me, thank you, and I love you." I asked him how would that make any difference to a mentally ill criminal who's sitting in a ward, in a room, while Dr. Hew Len is doing this in his own office, not even seeing the person, and addressing his petition to the Divine. How does that work?

We Are All Connected—We Are One

He says we're all connected; we are connected to the Divine. Basically, with those four phrases, he's saying, "I'm sorry, I have no idea what in me helped cocreate this person and that behavior. I have no idea. I'm sorry. I've been unaware. Please forgive me for not knowing how I participated." Because our beliefs are unconscious, we don't know, for the most part, what they are. You can find them, and I show you, in *The Missing Secret* and some of my other books, ways to investigate those, but you don't need to know them.

"I'm Sorry; Please Forgive Me; Thank You"

You're saying, "Please forgive me. I did not know. I was totally unaware." You're saying, "Thank you." Thank you shows incredible gratitude; it is an incredible motivator. It is connecting you to the Divine; you're thanking the Divine for taking care of this, for cleaning the beliefs, the negativity, the limitations. Dr. Hew Len was cleansing whatever programming had created these people in his life.

"I Love You"

The phrase *I love you*, to me, is the most powerful. It is the mantra that can change the planet. I've learned to do this so that it's my new self-talk. Instead of having the self-talk most of us have, which is very critical of ourselves and other people, my self-talk is now, "I'm sorry, please forgive me, thank you, I love you." I'm saying it to you right now with an awareness of the Divine as I say it.

Dr. Hew Len would say this *to the Divine,* repeatedly. He'd do it for every patient. Within a few months, these patients didn't have to be shackled. They didn't have to be sedated. Within six months, some of them were being released. Within two years, almost the entire ward had been released, pronounced as healed. No one expected these locked-up, mentally ill criminals to ever be released. Is this not amazing? Dr. Hew Len did it with something you and I can do: We can clean away those counterintentions by saying, "I want this house; I want this romance; I want this wealth; I want world peace; I want to . . . [fill in the blank]."

With the Divine's Help, Everything Can Be Erased

When you state your intention, and you realize that it's not happening yet, and you become impatient and frustrated and start to question everything and everyone, and you're wondering if there's something wrong with you, whatever those feelings are, whenever those come up for you, part of your awakening is to realize you can erase it all by taking it to the Divine.

Whatever you're feeling, take it to the Divine. When you're feeling it, you address your relationship to the Divine, whatever that means for you. "I'm sorry, please forgive me, thank you, and I love you. I'm sorry, please forgive me, thank you, and I love you." Is that not the simplest cleansing technique you've ever heard of? How many of you are already doing this?

Be Happy First

When people say they want things, like cars, houses, or anything else, there's a great deception going on. There's a great deception going on, and that deception is this: You think that when you get the car, the house, the relationship, the wealth, whatever you were going for, you'll be happy.

Your Point of Power: Happy Is Here Now

That's the great illusion. That's the great deception. You want to know why? Happiness is *right here*. I'm wearing this T-shirt, "Live in now," which I picked up at this convention. They're selling it at a booth, not my booth, but another one. *Live in now*. That is the secret. That is the real secret. I don't know that it's missing; it's right there in front of your face. It's pretty obvious. Part of this awakening is to realize that the point of power for you is right here in this moment.

A great thing that happens, a true miracle that happens, when you really get this. You look at this moment and you think, "Oh my God, look where I am; look at the people I'm with; look who I'm listening to; look at the people who are in the booths over here; look at everything that's going on in this whole facility. This is a miracle. This is a by-God miracle."

Miracles Are Happening in This Moment

Look what Judd is doing, the man who is putting on this event, by gathering all these people and all these great speakers. This is a miracle. It is happening here; it is happening now; but it's not just this now, this moment, this moment, this moment, it's all my miracles.

When you get that and you feel that you are present, you feel that you are here in the moment, that's when things happen in your life that will be so spectacular, you never could have imagined them before. And you couldn't imagine them before because your ego was doing the imagining. Your ego was saying, "Oh, I want this cool car." But the universe was saying, "I have this really spectacular car to give you, if you'd just give me a chance."

Perhaps you've focused on a particular relationship with a particular person. I hear that one a lot. "How do I get this one person to be attracted to me?" There are 6 billion people on the planet. Isn't there somebody who could be close to the quality you're looking for besides the one whom you've targeted? When you come from this moment, the magic and the miracles happen.

One of my favorite stories to tell is when I went on *Larry King* for the first time, and we were waiting in the outside security place, and some of my heroes were there. We were all standing around, excited, and we were getting our tags, going through security, and one of them slaps me on the back and says, "Isn't this fantastic? We're going on *Larry King*. I've been visualizing this for six years." I said, "Really? I've just been doing it for two weeks." Of course, I was kidding around with him, doing this macho thing, trying to one-up on him. We became good friends after that.

When the Universe Dials Your Number, Answer the Phone

The reality, though, the punch line that my friend doesn't know I'm telling you is . . . I *never* visualized it. Never, ever. I answered the phone, that was it, and I got on the plane. I took action and had a great time. The second time I was on the show, I hadn't visualized going back. It was cool to go on the first time. I mean, it's something to put in your scrapbook, right, *Larry King Live*?

The second time, I was contacted the night before to be on the show, live, the next night. I didn't visualize it; I didn't intend it. I answered the phone, said yes, and scrambled to get on a flight. I arrived early the next morning, did the show, and departed. Magic and miracles happen when you are in this moment.

Shhh . . . the Divine Is Talking

Some of you have read one of my early books, *The Attractor Factor,* and then later you read *Zero Limits,* and you express some confusion: "In *The Attractor Factor,* you talk about intentions, and the movie *The Secret* is all about intentions, but now you say, 'I've given up intentions.' So, what's the truth?" The truth of the matter is, I have not given up intentions—I've given up *ego* intentions. I do my best to come from what the Divine wants for me. In order for me to know what the Divine wants, I have to be here, in this moment.

Let the Divine Speak through You

I have a booth here, and some of you might have seen me hanging around the booth before coming onstage. You probably saw that I was a little nervous. Why was I a little nervous? I didn't have a clue what I was going to say. Nothing. I stood there while they were putting the mikes on me and a friend, who's around here someplace, and he said, "You doing okay? You know what you're going to talk about?" I said, "I got nothing."

Rhonda, who introduced me and who will be telling you about Miracles Coaching in a little bit, asked me what I would be talking about, and I said, "I never know. I'm going to be as surprised as everybody else when I get up here." That's because I have learned to come from the moment. Of course, I'm not totally there; otherwise, I wouldn't have been nervous. I wouldn't have had that little threat of fear, but I'm human and I'm admitting to you that it was there.

Now I'm onstage. I'm not nervous at all. I'm just letting it come through. What's coming through is taking me beyond what my ego would have said. My ego would have mapped out a speech. My ego would have had a PowerPoint presentation. My ego would have had all kinds of bullet points to go through for you. It probably would have been entertaining; it probably would have been useful; but I want to go on beyond that. I keep saying, "Life is a process of awakening." I'm in this process, too. I am awakening, too. We all are, we're in this together.

Let the Divine Drive—It Will Take You Beyond Your Wildest Dreams

Where I am at this point is to tell people, and to remind myself, that what you really want is here. When you come from here, the Divine will inspire you with what you want next. That's a Divine intention.

To give you a favorite example of mine, I do like cars, and I have a small car collection. If I wanted to have the largest car collection in the world, one so big that Jay Leno would be jealous and say, "Who the hell is this guy in Wimberley, Texas, who's got a bigger car collection than me?" And he'd want to come out here, and there'd be a little ego war about who has the best cars, who has the most cars, all of that. If I had that as a goal, it would be pure ego. Pure ego. The cars I have acquired have mostly come from inspiration—and often at the last minute.

You Can Trust in Inspired Action

Some of you know that I managed to attract the car that Steven Tyler of Aerosmith used to drive, an exotic race car made in 1998, a model that is no longer made, a car that Tyler drove and wrecked, at least twice. He had signed the car; it's a collectible. I found it on eBay in two hours before the auction was to close, and the person selling it didn't make a big deal about the fact that it had been owned by Steven Tyler. Something clicked inside me that said, "That is an investment opportunity: to have Steven Tyler's car, drive it for a little

while, and then sell it as "The Joe Vitale Secret, Steven Tyler . . ."
I don't know how long of a headline you can put on eBay, but my
musings came more from a fun place. They came from a detached
place. Another part of this missing secret is that you do want to clear
these counterintentions, and you can do so with a simple method
such as the ho'oponoponos, the Dr. Hew Len method: "I'm sorry.
Please forgive me. Thank you. I love you."

As you become more and more aware of where these intentions
are coming from, you'll get clearer about whether it's an ego intention. Notice that the ego seems like it's in the head, in the intellect,
in your thoughts. Or if it's coming more from the Divine, which
seems to be coming from your heart area. You can feel the difference
with practice, and if you don't know the difference, you keep cleaning. The cleaning is, "I'm sorry; please forgive me; thank you; I love
you. I'm sorry; please forgive me; thank you; I love you."

I think one of the problems people have is that they become too
attached to the end result. They think, "I have to have that particular
person," or they have to have that particular house, or they have to
have that particular job, or they have to have that particular amount of
money. That's when your ego is trying to control the situation, and
that's a limitation.

God Wants You to Be Abundant

The universe is trying to give you more. You have to let go of the
attachment, and people have asked me, "What does that mean?" You
want to come from a place of playfulness. "Wouldn't it be fun if I
had more clients? Wouldn't it be fun if I had this particular kind of
relationship? Wouldn't it be fun, wouldn't it be cool, wouldn't it be
fantastic if I had this particular house or vacation?" Fill in the blank.

Notice the difference, though. You're not attached to it. You're
not addicted to it. If you have the feeling that you will live or die

based on whether or not you get this thing, you're addicted to it. That addiction has an unconscious energy that is actually going to repel the object you seek. You have to have a playful energy. Wouldn't it be fun? Wouldn't it be cool?

I watched *The Big Idea with Donny Deutsch* on CNBC TV. How many of you have seen that show? I did want to go on his show. I love his show. Notice how I'm talking about it. I love his show. I admire him. I am inspired by him. Craig Perrine and I wrote a book called *Inspired Marketing*. We dedicated it to Donny Deutsch.

As you can see, I have a lot of respect, a lot of love, a lot of passion for him, and I was feeling as though I would love to go on his show. I just wanted to meet this man. I ended up going on the show, and it was a riot. I was so excited, I was like this little kid, sitting on the plane, squirming in my seat thinking, "Oh, I can't wait to get there. I'm going to meet Donny Deutsch. I'm going to meet Donny Deutsch." You know, I was 54, and I was acting like I was a 12-year-old.

The Secrets of the Universe Are Simpler than You Think

When I got there, I was so excited to meet him, and I did meet him, and they told me how long I'd be on the show: "You've got about four minutes to tell the secrets of the universe—four minutes. There's the camera; start talking."

Well I did it, but I wasn't addicted. I wasn't attached to it. It was a playful, passionate longing that said, "It would be fun to be on his show." That's the kind of mentality you want to have. These are all elements of what I call *The Missing Secret*. You want to keep clearing the counterintentions.

One of the best ways to clear the counterintentions, which many of you already know about, is, of course, ho'oponopono, the Dr. Hew Len method. "I'm sorry. Please forgive me. Thank you. I love you." That deserves your applause.

How many of you are familiar with EFT? A lot of you. That's the tapping method, and there's a DVD called *Try It on Everything.* They are selling it here, not at my booth, but I think in the back. If you wander around you'll see it, and you can tap away a lot of the beliefs that come up. Somebody throw a belief to me right now.

Your Level of Deservedness Matches Your Bank Account

"I'm not worthy" is a very popular belief. "I'm not worthy" is almost a universal feeling. In fact, almost all of us have what I call a level of deservedness within us that does not allow more good things. We push them away. This is an important insight. I've written about this, and I talk about it in my audio program *The Missing Secret.* You have a level of deservedness, a set point, based on your unconscious beliefs. Your feeling that "I'm not worthy" has been lodged in there for a long time. You can tap it away.

The DVD, *Try It on Everything,* explains it better, but I'll give you the short version. You take that belief, "I'm not worthy," and you tap the underside of the karate-chop part of your hand. Then you say, "Even though I'm not worthy, I deeply love, accept, and forgive myself."

In fact, let's all do that now. "Even though I'm not worthy, I deeply love, accept, and forgive myself. Even though I'm not worthy, I deeply love, accept, and forgive myself." By saying this, you're not anchoring the belief, you're actually releasing it. You're focusing on what you're going to release. You're tapping, and you're taking the belief and adding, "I deeply love, accept, and forgive myself."

Then you take it and tap the crown, "Not worthy." Tap above both eyes, "I'm not worthy." You tap under the nose, "I'm not worthy," under the lip, "I'm not worthy." I do this tapping technique every day. I did it before I came onstage. I told you I was a little nervous. I tapped it away. *Try It on Everything* shows you a clearing technique; the very name of the movie is telling you, "Try it on everything." No matter what's going on in your life, try it.

Ask for Help: Ask and Ye Shall Receive

Another way is to have a coach. I'm a great believer in having a coach. Look, folks, I was homeless 30-odd years ago. I told you about my Dallas years. When I got to Houston, I struggled in virtual poverty for another 10 years. I was a car salesman, a reporter, a laborer, a truck driver, a cab driver. I went through all kinds of things that I absolutely hated. I remember when I worked for an oil company, I cried going to work and going home because I was so profoundly unhappy.

How did I go from being a penniless, homeless, poverty-stricken guy to someone who collects rock-star cars, who lives a life of luxury, who spends almost every evening in my hot tub looking at the stars and saying, "Thank you for my life"? How did I get there?

It's one of the most common questions I get. I got here, first of all, because I'm always working on myself. I'm still working on myself. People who read my books can see the evolution of Joe Vitale, just by reading those different books.

I got here because I'm taking action; I am being persistent; I do have an intention; I am visualizing; I am reading all the time. Thank God for libraries. When I was homeless in Dallas, I went to libraries and read *The Magic of Believing*, Dale Carnegie's stuff, and many other volumes that helped me work on myself and find paths to move forward.

Yet, to be honest, all of that inched me forward very slowly. The thing that caused the quantum leap for me was having a coach. How many of you have a coach now? Quite a few of you do. A coach is somebody who can lovingly, joyfully, perceptively feed back to you your own beliefs. Because your beliefs are your beliefs, they seem like reality. You think they constitute reality. It's a belief-created reality. Change your beliefs and you get a different result.

I worked with a coach, and I talk about this in *The Attractor Factor*. I talk about it a little bit in my audio program *The Missing Secret*. By having a coach, I had somebody who was rooting for me, supporting me, encouraging me, and also shining a light on my beliefs in a joyful, nonjudgmental way. That was the number one thing that helped me shift.

You Can Change Your Beliefs: Just Decide

I'll give you a great example. I went through this whole phase, like most of us. Many of you might still be there. You think the more money you spend, the less money you have. Correct? No? You don't believe that one? How many believe that? The more money you spend, the less money you have. Doesn't that seem like good math? Isn't that what an accountant would say? Isn't that what the IRS would say? I used to believe that way. The more money I spent, the less I would have. I changed my belief. I changed it. A coach pointed out that it was a belief—not a reality. That's a belief. I'm calling it reality, yet it's only a belief.

The More Money I Spend, the More Money I Receive

Now my belief is this: The more money I spend, the more money I receive. I'll never be able to convince an accountant of that, but that's my reality. That is what happens to me. When I feel like buying something, it's in the back of my mind, "You know, if I go ahead and buy this, or if I donate to this particular cause, or start this particular movement and put a lot of money into it, many times that will come to me." It's my new belief. Because it's my new belief, it happens. It's the most astonishing thing. A coach helped me with that.

Now I'm going to invite Rhonda to talk about my Miracles Coaching program for a couple of minutes, and then I'll come back to wrap this up.

Rhonda: Thank you, Joe. I just want to say that this man is so inspiring, and I know that you've been moved by what he's said today. It's my great privilege to deliver the Miracles Coaching program. I work with some amazing people, and I'm inspired by this man every single day. I watch clients come into the program with a series of beliefs, just like Joe said.

They have an idea about what their life can look like. They have an idea about the limits of what's available to them, the abundance of what they can have in their life. They look for relationships; they look for success in business. They look for success in their families and with their children. They look for success physically. They're burdened with illness, and I've seen, time and time again, hundreds of people come through this program and have breakthroughs and miracles. Every single day they have the opportunity to learn from this man how to make those breakthroughs, how to stop believing those things that limit their lives.

We're going to be over at Joe's booth today. I have some of my colleagues with me, and if you have any questions about the Miracles Coaching program, please stop by and talk to us. We'd love to have an opportunity to tell you about it, and I just want to let you know that it's such a privilege to work with this man. Thank you for your time.

Everything You'll Ever Need Is in This Moment

Joe: Well, look, I'm going to sign off. I've been talking about *The Missing Secret*. I want you to know that the miracle is right now. The miracle is in this moment. If you can keep breathing, remember to live it now, be in this moment, and to take action, live out of this moment. Ideas will come to you, you'll be able to clear the blocks by always remembering, "I'm sorry. Please forgive me. Thank you. I love you." To help you remember that, I want you to know that I've been saying that again and again to you this whole time: I love you, I'm sorry, please forgive me, thank you, I love you, I'm sorry, please forgive me, thank you, I love you, I'm sorry, please forgive me, thank you, I love you all. Thank you.

Chapter 9

Special Bonus Report
Zero Limits *Answers*

This morning four hummingbirds sat around the outside feeder and drank in peace. This is amazing. Normally, hummingbirds fight with each other. They don't cooperate. They aren't at peace. They aren't loving.

Why are they all drinking together this morning?

Yesterday was the ending of the third live seminar on Zero Limits with me and Dr. Hew Len. It was one of the most loving and yet intense events of my life. Hundreds of people came from all over the world to experience it.

Dr. Hew Len revealed new cleaning methods, talked about deeper aspects of his way to the Divine, and more. I spoke of my own changes and revealed new stories.

We both took questions from the audience. Everyone left either feeling at peace or knowing how to get there.

Apparently that love spilled over to the hummingbirds. It's a wonderful metaphor and message: When you are at peace, the world becomes peaceful.

Ever since the 2007 publication of the best-selling book Zero Limits, written by me and Dr. Hew Len, people have had some key questions. I decided to answer the most common ones here.

May these questions and answers help lead you to peace—just like the hummingbirds.

Love,

Joe

1. I noticed that the order of the phrases are never the same. I've heard that the order matters, and then I hear that it doesn't. I'm afraid that I will do this wrong and that my misunderstanding of the process will adversely affect the outcome.

It doesn't matter what order you say the phrases in. The idea is to say them. Follow your inspiration and say them within yourself in the order that feels best. Let your feelings be your guide. In the last Zero Limits event, Dr. Hew shortened the four phrases to just two: "I love you" and "Thank you." Getting hung up on the phrases and anything about them is yet another thing to "clean" or "clear" on. The phrases are a simple tool to use as a cleaning device to help you work your way to Zero. That's all. Being afraid of doing them wrong is something to clean.

2. When I'm cleaning, who do I say it to? Me? The other person I'm cleaning on? I'm confused.

You never say it to the other person. What you are doing is cleaning the part of you that is perceiving the other person or object as a problem. It's never about anyone else or anything else. The outer object is the trigger that caused you to want to change something. Again, you don't want to change the outer. You want to change the inner. You use the clearing phrases to do that. You are addressing the Divine—no one else.

3. When I have a problem, and I do the cleaning, do I focus on the problem or the person while I'm cleaning? If my children have a problem and I want to clean for them, am I invading their personal space if they don't give me permission to clean on them first?

This is similar to the previous question. Again, you don't focus on the other person. You focus on *you*. The problem isn't "out there." It's in you. You focus on the problem as you experience it. You always experience it within yourself. As Dr. Hew Len has often asked, "Have you ever noticed that when you have a problem, you are there?" The point is that the problem is in *you*. That's where you put your focus. That's where you direct the cleaning. You are asking the Divine to remove the "energy" that you are feeling within yourself as you look out and see the "problem."

4. *Do I have to clean forever and ever for as long as I live? That seems tiring and like an awful lot of work. Is there another way?*

There is so much "data" in the world—programming, beliefs, negativity—that it's a lifelong challenge. Yes, you have to keep cleaning. But how hard is it, really, to say "I love you" and "Thank you" inside yourself?

5. *If all I need are the four phrases, then what's up with all these ho'oponopono products that people sell and profit from? If you ask me, capitalizing on spirituality is a turn-off and makes me question the validity of ho'oponopono. Can you please answer this for me?*

Thinking people are capitalizing on spirituality suggests that money is bad. Money is not bad. Money is, in fact, neutral. Money is even spiritual. I created an entire audio course about this issue (*The Secret to Attracting Money*). If everything is of the Divine, why would money be an exception? The products are there to help you. If you don't want them, don't buy them. But why sit in judgment when others are creating products to help you feel better, get clearer, and be happier? They are doing you a service. Judging it as "bad" or "unspiritual" sounds like a limiting belief that needs to be cleared. It sounds self-righteous. I'll clean on it.

6. *How do we teach others to clean?*

You don't. No one else needs to know anything about clearing. Only you do. Dr. Hew Len has spent the past 25 years cleaning himself. He openly says the only reason he is alive is to clean. It doesn't matter if anyone else does it. It matters that *you* do it. One of the things I hear at events is people listening to the problems of others and then advising them, "You should clean on that." Wrong. Whenever you hear a problem, it's *yours* to clean on. Just start doing the cleaning right then and there. In fact, you should never tell anyone to "clean on it." Whatever you hear or experience is *yours* to clean on.

7. *I've been to a* Zero Limits *event and I still don't get it. What's this all about?*

Basically, this is about returning to Divinity. In my audio program, *The Awakening Course,* I introduce four stages of awakening. Most people never leave the first one (victimhood). Thanks to movies like *The Secret* and *The Compass,* many people are getting to level two (empowerment). Thanks to the book *Zero Limits,* some are aware of level three (surrender). But there's also a fourth level. That's where you "awaken" to Divinity. That's where the Divine consciously breathes *through* you. *Zero Limits* is a way to clear out all the "data" (or head stuff) that stands between you and the Divine ("Zero"). So, what's this all about? It's about getting clear of the static in your mind so the Divine lives *through* you with awareness and love. To get there, we have a lot of work to do. So, keep cleaning.

8. *Did this method ever work for you, personally? Did it heal you or anyone close to you? Do you ever get to zero??*

The only goal of cleaning is to help you erase the garbage that's between you and the Divine. As you clean, you may get a healing or some other result. But that's not the goal. The intention is to get to Zero, which is the place where the Divine lives through you. When Dr. Hew Len worked with the patients in that mental hospital for the criminally insane, he didn't work to heal them, he worked to heal himself. Obviously, it worked. I've been doing the cleaning for almost four years now. I do it nonstop. Why? So I can keep cleaning the interference between me and the Divine. One day, if the

Divine so wants it, I will be at Zero. Until then, I keep cleaning. I wouldn't keep doing it if it didn't work. To offer some evidence that this method works, here's an e-mail I received one day:

> I read your book *Zero Limits* in December, 2008. I work as a life-coach and parenting instructor at the Women's prison in Baton Rouge. I hold three classes each week with 20 women in each class. I started doing the ho'oponopono immediately after starting the book. I could see instant results with the women in the group. I shared the information with them and bought five books for them to take turns reading. They have shared so many success stories with me about how the deputies in charge of them are changing. One day last week, there was some sort of disturbance going on in the prison. I could hear the commotion outside of my classroom. The warden stepped in my classroom and had this stunned look on his face. He couldn't believe the calmness and quietness of the room with all of the ruckus going on outside. He told me, "I don't know what you are doing, just keep doing it." He has shared with me on several occasions that all of the women are behaving better and are actually getting to have privileges they have never been able to have before. I am also having positive changes with my teenage daughters and husband. Thank you so much for bringing this information to light.
>
> Cindy Ray-Huber
> Regional Director, RCB of Baton Rouge
> www.lifecoach123.com

9. What's the difference between Zero Limits *seminars and ho'oponopono basic and advanced courses? Do I have to attend any of these first, before taking the next class? If this information is to be made private, how come you are allowed to reveal some of the secrets in* Zero Limits *or release recordings of your* Zero Limits *events?*

The main difference between a *Zero Limits* event and a ho'oponopono basic event is this: With *Zero Limits,* you get me as the coinstructor. You have to take the basic ho'oponopono course and practice the methods you learn for at least two years before you can take an advanced ho'oponopono course. I was permitted to release some of the information because Dr. Hew Len gave me that permission. He is, after all, the coauthor of *Zero Limits* and the main instructor of ho'oponopono. If he says I can write a book or release audios or DVDs, then of course I can.

10. *"I am sorry!" Does this mean apology or sadness? What do I have to be sorry for when everything in the universe is perfect? I don't like having to say it.*

You need to say "I'm sorry" and "Please forgive me" for being unconscious. It has nothing to do with regret, guilt, shame, or blame, but everything to do with realizing you've been asleep. When you bump into someone in the store, you say "I'm sorry." Why? Because you made a mistake. You were unconscious and did something while you were unaware. When you address the Divine and say those phrases, you are letting the Divine know you were unconscious. Forgiveness is one of the most powerful transformative tools you have. If you aren't willing to ask for forgiveness for being unconscious, you are probably blocking the Divine's flow in your life in other areas, too. Having said all that, I once asked Dr. Hew Len what to tell people who complained about saying "I am sorry." He said, "Tell them they don't have to say it."

Bibliography

If you want to awaken, you must continue to learn and grow. Here are many great books (and a few audio recordings) to help you along your path to freedom. Your library or local bookstore or Amazon .com will have these.

Allen, James. *As a Man Thinketh*. Los Angeles, CA: Tarcher Books, 2008.

Assaraf, John. *The Answer*. New York: Atria Books, 2008.

Atkinson, William Walter. *Thought Vibration, or The Law of Attraction in the Thought World*. Chicago: New Thought Publishing, 1906.

Ball, Ron, et al. *Freedom at Your Fingertips*. Fredericksburg, VA: InRoads Publishing, 2006.

Barrett, Rick, and Joe Vitale. *Give to Live*. www.givetolivebook.com, 2008.

Beckwith, Michael Bernard. *Spiritual Liberation*. New York: Atria Books, 2009.

Behrend, Genevieve, and Joe Vitale. *How to Attain Your Desires by Letting Your Subconscious Mind Work for You, Vol. 1*. Garden City, NY: Morgan-James Publishing, 2004.

———. *How to Attain Your Desires, Vol. 2: How to Live Life and Love It!* Garden City, NY: Morgan-James Publishing, 2005.

Bender, Sheila Sidney, and Mary Sise. *The Energy of Belief: Psychology's Power Tools to Focus Intention and Release Blocking Beliefs*. Santa Rosa, CA: Energy Psychology Press, 2008.

Bowen, Will. *A Complaint Free World*. New York: Doubleday, 2007.

Braden, Gregg. *The Divine Matrix: Bridging Time, Space, Miracles, and Belief*. Carlsbad, CA: Hay House, 2006.

Bristol, Claude. *The Magic of Believing*. New York: Pocket Books, 1991.

Bruce, Alexandra. *Beyond the Secret*. New York: Disinformation Company, 2007.

Butterworth, Eric. *Spiritual Economics: The Principles and Process of True Prosperity*. Lee's Summit, MO: Unity, 1993.

Byrne, Rhonda. *The Secret*. New York: Atria Books/Beyond Words, 2006.

Callahan, Roger. *Tapping the Healer Within: Using Thought-Field Therapy to Instantly Conquer Your Fears, Anxieties, and Emotional Distress*. New York: McGraw-Hill, 2002.

Canfield, Jack, and Janet Switzer. *The Success Principles: How to Get from Where You Are to Where You Want to Be*. New York: Harper Collins, 2006.

Casey, Karen. *Change Your Mind and Your Life Will Follow*. New York: Conari Press, 2005.

Chopra, Deepak. *The Spontaneous Fulfillment of Desire*. New York: Harmony, 2003.

Coates, Denise. *Feel It Real! The Magical Power of Emotions*. New York: Atria Books, 2006.

Collins, Marva, and Civia Tamarkin. *Marva Collins' Way*. Los Angeles: J.P. Tarcher, 1990.

Coppel, Paula Godwin. *Sacred Secrets: Finding Your Way to Joy, Peace and Prosperity*. Unity Village, MO: Unity House, 2008.

Cornyn-Selby, Alyce. *What's Your Sabotage?* Portland, OR: Beynch Press, 2000.

Craig, K. C. *Placing Your Order: Steps for Successful Manifestations*. Fairfax, VA: RMS Publications, 2007.

Dahl, Lynda Madden. *Beyond the Winning Streak: Using Conscious Creation to Consistently Win at Life*. Portland, OR: Woodbridge Group, 2000.

———. *Ten Thousand Whispers: A Guide to Conscious Creation*. Portland, OR: Woodbridge Group,1995.

———. *The Wizards of Consciousness: Making the Imponderable Practical*. Portland, OR: Woodbridge Group,1997.

Deutschman, Alan. *Change or Die: The Three Keys to Change at Work and in Life*. New York: Reagan Books, 2007.

Di Marsico, Bruce. *The Option Method: Unlock Your Happiness with Five Simple Questions*. Walnut Grove, CA: Dragonfly Press, 2006.

Doré, Carole. *The Emergency Handbook for Getting Money Fast!* San Francisco: Celestial Arts, 2002.

Doyle, Bob. *Wealth Beyond Reason*. Duluth, GA: Boundless Living, 2004.

Dwoskin, Hale. *The Sedona Method: Your Key to Lasting Happiness Success, Peace and Emotional Well-Being*. Sedona, AZ: Sedona Press, 2003.

Dyer, Wayne. *The Power of Intention: Learning to Co-Create Your World Your Way*. Carlsbad, CA: Hay House, 2004.

Eker, T. Harv. *Secrets of the Millionaire Mind: Mastering the Inner Game of Wealth*. New York: HarperCollins, 2005.

Ellsworth, Paul. *Mind Magnet: How to Unify and Intensify Your Natural Faculties for Efficiency, Health and Success*. Holyoke, MA: Elizabeth Towne Company, 1924.

Evans, Mandy. *Emotional Options: A Handbook for Happiness*. New York: Morgan James, 2004.

———. *Travelling Free: How to Recover from the Past*. Encinitas, CA: Yes You Can Press, 2005.

Fengler, Fred, and Varnum, Todd. *Manifesting Your Heart's Desires, Book I and Book II*. Burlington, VT: HeartLight, 2002.

Ferguson, Bill. *Heal the Hurt that Sabotages Your Life*. Houston, TX: Return to the Heart, 2004.

Fisher, Mark. *The Instant Millionaire: A Tale of Wisdom and Wealth*. New San Francisco: World Library, 1993.

Ford, Debbie. *The Dark Side of the Light Chasers*. New York: Riverhead Books, 1998.

———. *Why Good People Do Bad Things: How to Stop Being Your Own Worst Enemy*. New York: HarperOne, 2008.

Gage, Randy. *Why You're Dumb, Sick & Broke . . . And How to Get Smart, Healthy & Rich!* Hoboken, NJ: John Wiley & Sons, 2006.

Gaines, Edwene. *The Four Spiritual Laws of Prosperity*. Emmaus, PA: Rodale Press, 2005.

Gillett, Dr. Richard. *Change Your Mind, Change Your World*. New York: Simon & Schuster, 1992.

Gilmore, Ehryck. *The Law of Attraction 101*. Chicago: Eromlig Publishing, 2006.

Goi, James. *How to Attract Money Using Mind Power*. West Conshohocken, PA: Infinity Publishing, 2007.

Goldberg, Bruce. *Karmic Capitalism: A Spiritual Approach to Financial Independence*. Baltimore, MD: Publish America, 2005.

Grabhorn, Lynn. *Excuse Me, Your Life Is Waiting: The Astonishing Power of Feelings*. Charlottsville, VA: Hampton Roads, 2003.

Gregory, Eva. *The Feel Good Guide to Prosperity*. San Francisco: LifeCoaching, 2005.

Hall, Philip. *Jesus Taught It, Too: The Early Roots of the Law of Attraction*. Alberta, Canada: Avatar, 2007.

Hamilton, Roger. *Your Life, Your Legacy*. Achievers International, 2006

Harris, Bill. *Thresholds of the Mind: Your Personal Roadmap to Success, Happiness, and Contentment*. Beaverton, OR: Centerpoint Research, 2002.

Hartong, Leo. *Awakening to the Dream*. Salisburg, United Kingdom: Non-Duality Press, 2003.

Hawkins, David. *Devotional Nonduality*. Sedona, AZ: Veritas Publishing, 2006.

———. *Healing and Recovery*. Sedona, AZ: Veritas Publishing, 2009.

———. *I: Reality and Subjectivity*. Sedona, AZ: Veritas Publishing, 2003.

———. *Power vs. Force: The Hidden Determinants of Human Behavior*. Carlsbad, CA: Hay House, 2002.

———. *Transcending the Levels of Consciousness*. Sedona, AZ: Veritas Publishing, 2006.

Helmstetter, Shad. *Self-Talk Solution*. New York: Pocket Books, 1987.

———. *What to Say When You Talk to Yourself*. New York: Pocket Books, 1982.

Hicks, Jerry and Esther. *Ask and It Is Given: Learning to Manifest Your Desires*. Carlsbad, CA: Hay House, 2004.

———. *The Law of Attraction: the Basics of the Teachings of Abraham*. Carlsbad, CA: Hay House, 2006.

———. *Money and the Law of Attraction*. Carlsbad, CA: Hay House, 2008.

Hill, Napoleon. *Think and Grow Rich*. New York: Fawcett Books, 1935.

Holmes, Ernest. *Creative Mind and Success*. San Francisco: Tarcher, 2004.

———. *Science of Mind*. San Francisco: Tarcher, 1998.

Houlder, Kulananda and Dominic. *Mindfulness and Money*. New York: Broadway, 2002.

Kahler, Rick, and Kathleen Fox. *Conscious Finance: Uncover Your Hidden Money Beliefs and Transform the Role of Money in Your Life*. Rapid City, SD: FoxCraft, 2005.

Katie, Bryon. *Loving What Is: Four Questions That Can Change Your Life*. New York: Harmony Books, 2002.

Kaufman, Barry Neil. *To Love Is to Be Happy With*. New York: Fawcett, 1985.

Kennedy, Dan. *No B.S. Marketing to the Affluent* (Foreword by Joe Vitale). Newburgh, NY: Entrepreneur Press, 2008.

———. *No B.S. Wealth Attraction for Entrepreneurs*. Newburgh, NY: Entrepreneur Press, 2010.

Landrum, Gene. *The Superman Syndrome—The Magic of Myth in the Pursuit of Power: The Positive Mental Moxie of Myth for Personal Growth*. Lincoln, NE: iUniverse, 2005.

Lapin, Rabbi Daniel. *Thou Shall Prosper: Ten Commandments for Making Money*. Hoboken, NJ: John Wiley & Sons, 2002.

Lapin, Jackie. *The Art of Conscious Creation*. Charleston, SC: Elevate, 2007.

Larson, Christian D. *Your Forces and How to Use Them*. London: Fowler, 1912.

Larson, Melody. *The Beginner's Guide to Abundance*. Booklocker.com, 2007.

Levenson, Lester. *The Ultimate Truth About Love & Happiness: A Handbook for Life*. Sherman Oaks, CA: Lawrence Crane Enterprises, 2003.

Lipton, Bruce. *The Biology of Belief: Unleashing the Power of Consciousness, Matter and Miracles*. Atlanta, GA: Mountain of Love, 2005.

Losier, Michael. *Law of Attraction.* Victoria, Canada: Losier Publications, 2003.

Love, Lisa. *Beyond the Secret: Spiritual Power and the Law of Attraction.* Charlottesville, VA: Hampton Roads, 2007.

Mackenzie, Kathleen. *Not Manifesting? This Book Is for You!* Denver, CO: Outskirts Press, 2007.

Martin, Art. *Your Body Is Talking; Are You Listening?* Penryn, CA: Personal Transformation, 2001.

McTaggart, Lynne. *The Intention Experiment: Using Your Thoughts to Change Your Life and the World.* New York: Free Press, 2007.

Miller, Carolyn. *Creating Miracles: Understanding the Experience of Divine Intervention.* Tiboron, CA: H.J. Kramer Inc.,1995.

Miller, Scott. *Until It's Gone.* Vancouver, WA: AHA! Press, 2008.

————. *The Power of Your Subconscious Mind.* New York: Bantam, 2001.

Neville, Goddard. *Immortal Man: A Compilation of Lectures.* Camarillo, CA: DeVorss & Company, 1984.

Neville, Goddard, and Joe Vitale. *At Your Command.* Garden City, NY: Morgan-James Publishing, 2005.

Norville, Deborah. *Thank You Power: Making the Science of Gratitude Work for You.* Nashville, TN: Thomas Nelson, 2007.

Oates, Robert. *Permanent Peace: How to Stop Terrorism and War—Now and Forever.* Fairfield, VA: Oates, 2002.

O'Bryan, Pat, and Joe Vitale. *The Myth of Passive Income: The Problem and the Solution.* E-book, 2004. www.mythofpassiveincome.com.

————. *Think and Grow Rich Workbook,* a free e-book based on the classic by Napoleon Hill. E-book, 2004. www.InstantChange.com.

Patterson, Kerry. *Influencers: The Power to Change Anything.* New York: McGraw-Hill, 2008.

Pauley, Tom. *I'm Rich Beyond My Wildest Dreams, I Am, I Am, I Am.* New York: Rich Dreams, 1999.

Pavlina, Steve. *Personal Development for Smart People.* Carlsbad, CA: Hay House, 2008.

Pilzer, Paul Zane. *God Wants You to Be Rich.* New York: Touchstone Faith, 2007.

Ponder, Catherine. *The Dynamic Laws of Prosperity.* Amarillo, TX: DeVorss, 1985.

Proctor, Bob. *It's Not About the Money.* Toronto: Burman Books, 2008.

————. *You Were Born Rich: Now You Can Discover and Develop Those Riches.* Toronto, Canada: LifeSuccess Productions, 1997.

Rahula, Bhikkhu Basnagoda. *The Buddha's Teachings on Prosperity.* Somerville, MA: Wisdom Publications, 2008.

Rafter, Mark. *The Wealth Manifesto: Transforming Your Life from Survive to Thrive*. Auburn, CA: New Knowledge Press, 2008.

Ressler, Peter, and Mitchell, Monika. *Spiritual Capitalism: How 9/11 Gave Us Nine Spiritual Lessons of Work and Business*. New York: Chilmark Books, 2007.

Rhinehart, Luke. *The Book of est*. Austin, TX: Hypnotic Marketing, Inc., 2010. www.bookofest.com.

Ritt, Michael, and Landers, Kirk. *A Lifetime of Riches: The Biography of Napoleon Hill*. New York: Dutton, 1995.

Roazzi, Vincent. *Spirituality of Success: Getting Rich with Integrity*. Dallas, TX: Namaste, 2001.

Roberts, Jane. *The Nature of Personal Reality: Specific, Practical Techniques for Solving Everyday Problems and Enriching the Life You Know*. New York: New World Library, 1994.

Rutherford, Darel. *So, Why Aren't You Rich?* Albuquerque, NM: Dar, 1998.

Ryce, Michael. *Why Is This Happening to Me—Again?* Theodosia, MO: Ryce, 1996.

Sage, Carnelian. *The Greatest Manifestation Principle in the World*. Beverley Hills, CA: Think Outside the Book, 2007.

Scheinfeld, Robert. *Busting Loose from the Money Game: Mind-Blowing Strategies for Changing the Rules of a Game You Can't Win*. Hoboken, NJ: John Wiley & Sons, 2006.

Shumsky, Susan. *Miracle Prayer: Nine Steps to Creating Prayers That Get Results*. Berkeley, CA: Celestial Arts, 2006.

Siebold, Steve. *177 Mental Toughness Secrets of the World Class*. Clearwater, FL: London House Press, 2005.

Staples, Dr. Walter Doyle. *Think Like a Winner!* Hollywood, CA: Wilshire, 1993.

Tipping, Colin. *Radical Manifestation: The Fine Art of Creating the Life You Want*. Marietta, GA: Global 13 Publications, 2006.

Truman, Karol. *Feelings Buried Alive Never Die. . .* Olympus, UT: Brigham Distributing, 1991.

Vitale, Joe. *Adventures Within: Confessions of an Inner World Journalist*. Author House, 2003.

———. *Attract Money Now*. E-book, 2010. www.attractmoneynowbook .com.

———. *The Attractor Factor: Five Easy Steps for Creating Wealth (or Anything Else) from the Inside Out*. Hoboken, NJ: John Wiley & Sons, 2005. Revised, 2008.

———. *The Awakening Course*. Audio program. Austin, TX: Hypnotic Marketing, Inc., 2008. www.awakeningdownload.com.

————. *Buying Trances: A New Psychology of Sales and Marketing*. Hoboken, NJ: John Wiley & Sons, 2007.

————. *Expect Miracles*. Toronto, Canada: Burman Books, 2008.

————. *The Greatest Money-Making Secret in History*. 1st New York: Books Library, 2003.

————. *Hypnotic Writing*. Hoboken, NJ: John Wiley & Sons, 2007.

————. *The Key: The Missing Secret to Attracting Whatever You Want*. Hoboken, NJ: John Wiley & Sons, 2007.

————. *Life's Missing Instruction Manual: The Guidebook You Should Have Been Given at Birth*. Hoboken, NJ: John Wiley & Sons, 2006.

————. *The Missing Secret: How to Use the Law of Attraction to Get Whatever You Want, Every Time*. Audio program. Niles, IL: Nightingale-Conant, 2008.

————. *The Power of Outrageous Marketing!* Audio program. Niles, IL: Nightingale-Conant, 1998.

————. *The Secret to Attracting Money*. Audio program. Niles, IL: Nightingale-Conant, 2009.

————. *The Seven Lost Secrets of Success*. Hoboken, NJ: John Wiley & Sons, 2007.

————. *There's a Customer Born Every Minute: P.T. Barnum's Amazing 10 "Rings of Power" for Creating Fame, Fortune, and a Business Empire Today—Guaranteed!* Hoboken, NJ: John Wiley & Sons, 2006.

Vitale, Joe, and Ihaleakala Hew Len. *Zero Limits: The Secret Hawaiian System for Wealth, Health, Peace, and More*. Hoboken, NJ: John Wiley & Sons, 2007.

Vitale, Joe, and Bill Hibbler. *Meet and Grow Rich*. Hoboken, NJ: John Wiley & Sons, 2006.

Vitale, Joe, with Craig Perrine. *Inspired Marketing*. Hoboken, NJ: John Wiley & Sons, 2008.

Vitale, Joe, and Mark Ryan. *Attracting Wealth: Magnetizing Your Unconscious Mind for Prosperity: Subliminal Manifestation*, DVD #4. Austin, TX: Hypnotic I Media, Inc., 2007. www.subliminalmanifestation.com.

Waldroop, James, and Timothy Butler. *The 12 Bad Habits That Hold Good People Back*. New York: Random House, 2000.

————. *The Science of Getting Rich*. New York: Penquin/Tarcher, 2007.

Wenger, Win, and Richard Poe. *The Einstein Factor: A Proven New Method for Increasing Your Intelligence*. Roseville, CA: Prima, 1996.

Wilde, Stuart. *The Trick to Money Is Having Some*. Carlsbad, CA: Hay House, 1995.

Wojton, Djuna. *Karmic Healing: Clearing Past-Life Blocks to Present-Day Love, Health and Happiness*. Berkeley, CA: Crossing Press, 2006.

Wright, Kurt. *Breaking the Rules*. Boise, ID: CPM, 1998.

About the Author

Dr. Joe Vitale, one of the standout stars in the hit movie *The Secret,* is the author of far too many books to list here. He wrote the best-sellers, *The Attractor Factor: 5 Easy Steps for Creating Wealth (or Anything Else) from the Inside Out; Zero Limits;* and *Attract Money Now.* He also wrote *Life's Missing Instruction Manual: The Guidebook You Should Have Been Given at Birth.* In addition, he wrote *Hypnotic Writing* and *Buying Trances: A New Psychology of Sales and Marketing.* Besides all of his books, Joe recorded the number one best-selling Nightingale-Conant audio programs, *The Power of Outrageous Marketing, The Secret to Attracting Money,* and *The Missing Secret.* He is the creator of Miracles Coaching, too. His main web sites are www.mrfire.com and www.JoeVitale.com.

Special Miracles Coaching Offer
Free Session

For the past 25 years Dr. Joe Vitale has helped people like you attract *all* kinds of miracles in *every* area of their lives. He's helped people attract . . .

- Money
- Cars
- Soul mates
- Better health
- New careers
- Dream homes
- Awakenings

The list goes on and on! And Dr. Vitale can help you do the same in his new *Joe Vitale's Miracles Coaching Program*™! The key is for you to be ready. (And it looks like you are or you would not be reading this right now.) If you want to learn more about how you can attract money, jobs, health, love, careers, relationships, or anything else quickly, sign up now, or experience a free sample, by going to . . .

www.MiraclesCoaching.com

At this site, you can also see a short film about Miracles Coaching and listen to an in-depth interview with a Miracles Coach.

Index

LIBRARY
PALO ALTO CITY

www.cityofpaloalto.org/library